THE ACTIV

BIBLE

THE ACTIVITY BIBLE

Stories by Leena Lane

Illustrations by Graham Round

Equipping the Church

Published in the UK by Equipping the Church, a brand of Kingsway CLC Trust,
Unit 5 Glendale Avenue, Sandycroft, Deeside, CH5 2QP.

ISBN: 9781803760186

Kingsway CLC Trust is a Charity, Number 265612, and a Limited Company
registered in England, Registration Number 1093879.

This edition 2024

Publishing Director: Annette Reynolds
Puzzle checker: Ben Reynolds
Art Director: Gerald Rogers
Pre-production: Kev Holt, GingerPromo

Printed in China

Presented to: ______________________

From: ______________________

Date: ______________________

CONTENTS

Old Testament

New Testament

THE OLD TESTAMENT

THE BEAUTIFUL GARDEN

At the beginning of time, the world was dark and empty.

Then God spoke into the darkness.

'Let there be light!' He commanded.

Light appeared and God was pleased with what He saw. He made day and night, to separate the light and the darkness.

God made sky above the earth. He made huge mountains, valleys and rolling hills. He made the deep blue sea.

God made plants and flowers and trees, with juicy fruit, prickles and leaves. He made wheat, barley and oats.

God made stars in the sky. He made

planets, the red-hot sun and the silvery moon.

Then came a very exciting moment! God filled the sea with slippery, shiny fish and the air with birds that chatter and sing. God made animals that leap and clamber and crawl on the land.

God was pleased with everything He had made. It was very good.

'Now I will make human beings,' said God. 'They will look after the world I have made and all the animals in it. They will eat the juicy fruit and the ripe grain of the fields.'

God made the first man, called Adam. He took some soil and blew the breath of life into him. Then He made a woman, called Eve, to be Adam's companion.

God wanted them to enjoy His world. He wanted them to be happy. God loved them very much. He made a beautiful garden for them to live in. It was called the Garden of Eden.

God looked at all He had made and was pleased with His creation. It was a good world.

WORD SEARCH

Below there are a lot of jumbled up letters.
Hidden among them are ten words from
the story of creation.
Find the ten words and cross them out below.

J O K U S K Y S B H U E A R T H B G H J S E A B T H H E V E
P L A N T S B N T R E E S N J K L U B I R D S F A N I M A L S
F I S H J U I K S H A S B H U J H I U L N A D A M N B M I P

Now put a ring around those words hidden in the grid. They could be written up, down, across or backwards!

S	U	P	L	A	N	T	S
O	K	P	J	K	N	E	D
E	B	Y	C	X	A	V	R
A	I	A	D	A	M	E	I
R	G	S	E	E	R	T	B
T	O	F	I	S	H	E	R
H	N	B	P	O	J	U	R
I	S	L	A	M	I	N	A

Opposites

Choose a word from the list below and match it with its opposite from the column on the right by drawing a line between them.

HAPPY	LIGHT
DARK	FULL
EMPTY	SEA
LOVE	SAD
SAND	HATE

THE ENEMY IN THE GARDEN

Adam and Eve were very happy living in the beautiful garden.

God asked them to choose names for the animals and to take care of them. The garden was full of delicious fruits and vegetables, and they could eat anything they wanted, except from one tree.

There was a big tree in the middle of the garden. God told them about it:

'It is called the Tree of Knowing Good and Bad. You mustn't eat any of its fruit. If you do, everything will be spoiled.'

One day, God's enemy came into the garden. He didn't like the beautiful garden and he wanted to spoil all the things God had made and planned.

He crept up to Eve and hissed in her ear.

'Listen to me. God was lying when He told you about that tree. You won't die if you eat its fruit. You will be great, just like God! You will know all that He knows.'

Eve looked at the tree. The fruit looked so delicious. She took a big, deep bite. Then she gave some to Adam.

Suddenly they knew what they had done. They didn't feel the same anymore.

Everything was spoiled. They had disobeyed God.

Adam and Eve made themselves clothes out of fig leaves. Then they hid.

When God came to the garden to talk to His friends, He called out to them.

'Where are you?'

But they were afraid to talk to God. They felt guilty because they had disobeyed Him. Then they tried to blame each other.

God was very sad.

'Because you did not trust Me,' He told them, 'you will have to leave the beautiful garden. We can no longer walk and talk together as friends.'

So Adam and Eve went from the Garden of Eden and did not return.

FIND AND COUNT

There are five differences between these pictures. Can you make a circle around each one you can find?

PICTURE QUIZ

Look at the pictures on pages 14-15 then answer the questions

How many birds are in the garden?	
How many animals are in the garden?	
How many 'pairs of eyes' can you count?	
How many trees can you count?	
How many flowers can you count?	

WORD PUZZLE

Fit the missing letters into the words listed below.

Then put a ring around those words hidden in the grid. They could be written up, down, across or backwards!

BEA _ T _ _ UL

_ NIM _ _ S

G _ _ DE _

T _ E _

BI _ _

_ O _

S _ _ P _ N _

F _ UI _ _

VE _ _ TA _ _ E _

_ D _ M

_ V _

B	E	A	U	T	I	F	U	L	S
Y	G	J	E	B	V	C	D	S	E
G	U	P	O	V	B	T	R	T	L
C	A	D	A	M	E	N	I	I	B
K	M	R	L	M	E	E	B	U	A
O	Y	U	D	V	R	P	E	R	T
X	C	E	T	E	T	R	V	F	E
H	W	T	B	V	N	E	D	O	G
A	N	I	M	A	L	S	K	I	E
B	E	B	W	O	P	L	J	H	V

THE TRIPLE-DECKER BOAT

God was sad. The beautiful world He had made was ruined. People had become evil and were fighting each other.

There was only one good man left. He was called Noah. He had a wife and three grown-up sons, Shem, Ham and Japheth.

God spoke to Noah. 'I will destroy the people on the earth! But I promise to save you and your family. This is how you will be safe: you must build a large boat from wood. Make it a triple-decker, with a door at the front. Coat it with tar to keep out the water. I am going to flood the earth and wash everything away!

'Take into the boat all your family and two of every kind of animal on the earth. We will keep them alive. Take food for your family and the animals.'

Noah did as God told him and built a huge triple-decker boat.

Noah was six hundred years old when the flood came. He and his family went into the boat, along with a male and female of every kind of animal and bird.

God shut the door.

The rain began to fall and the earth was flooded. The boat floated on the waters.

'Hold on tight, everybody!' shouted Noah. 'And don't panic! God will keep us safe!'

WHICH ANIMAL IS THIS?

Noah took lots of different animals into his boat when it was built. See how many you can identify and tick the right box.

Is this:

A tiger?

A lion?

Is this:

A cow?

A horse?

Is this:

A goat?

A sheep?

Are these:

Monkeys?

Gorillas?

Is this:

An ostrich?

An eagle?

Find the Word

Written below are ten words from the story of The Triple-Decker Boat, but they are all anagrams. Rearrange the letters to find the words and write them in the box. Then ring the words in the grid. Remember, they may be written in any direction!

SILENT	
DOG	
DAME	
SHAW	
PEEK	
RAT	
NEED	
RAG END	
VASE	
MITE	

G	O	D	H	O	P	K
V	A	B	X	M	I	T
E	F	R	N	C	Z	P
R	A	C	D	N	E	X
T	M	A	D	E	W	J
Z	U	I	K	T	N	A
F	G	H	E	S	E	E
C	V	V	U	I	D	M
W	A	S	H	L	E	I
S	L	K	O	K	M	T

RAIN, RAIN AND MORE RAIN

It rained and rained and rained. It rained like it had never rained before. The earth was flooded. There was nothing left to see. No trees, no fields, no houses, no people. It had all been washed away.

Noah and the animals were safe in the boat. They had enough food to last them for a long time.

'I wonder when the rain will stop?' asked one of Noah's sons. 'Surely this can't go on for very much longer!'

Then God made a strong wind blow and the water on the earth began to go down. The rain stopped. It took a hundred and fifty days for the water to run back into the soggy ground.

Noah waited for the boat to come to rest on a bit of land. There was nothing in sight at first. Nothing but water all around. Then at last the mountaintops appeared!

Noah sent a raven out of the boat. It flew round and round until the water had gone down. Noah sent out a dove, but it found no place to rest and flew back to Noah. A week later Noah sent the dove

out again. This time it returned with an olive branch in its beak. It had found a tree!

At last, God called Noah, saying, 'Leave the boat, you and your family and all the animals. Fill the land with the birds and animals. Have children and fill the earth again.'

God put a beautiful rainbow in the sky, a huge stripy archway of red, orange, yellow, green, blue, indigo and violet. Noah and his family had never seen anything so wonderful.

'This rainbow is a sign of My promise,' God said. 'I will never again destroy all living things on the earth with a flood. Never again will a great flood destroy the whole earth. I make this promise to you and to all living things on the earth.'

TWO OF EACH KIND

Noah selected pairs of animals to enter the ark. Can you copy the animals below, square by square, to make three pairs?

WHAT'S WRONG WITH THE STORY?

Can you find seven mistakes in the story extract below? There is one mistake on each line.

Jonah waited for the triple-decker boat to come to rest on a bit of paper. There was nothing in sight at first. Nothing but sheep all around. Then at last the mountaintops appeared!

Noah sent a eagle out of the boat. It flew round and round until the water had gone down. Noah sent out a dove, but it found no place to rest and swam back to Noah. A week later Noah sent the dove out again. This time it returned with a banana branch in its beak. It had found a supermarket!

SPIDERS

How many spiders are hiding in the big picture above?

ABRAM'S JOURNEY

A long time after the time of Noah, when people had again begun to live on the land and make their homes there, God spoke to a man called Abram.

'I want you to leave your home and your country. Leave behind the people you grew up with and the land that belonged to your father. I want you to go to a land that I will show you. I will bless you there and make a great nation from your family.'

Abram believed God. He was not a very young man. He was already seventy-five years old. But he set off with his wife Sarai and his nephew, Lot. They had lots of servants and lots of camels and donkeys, sheep and goats. They packed up everything they had and started their long journey. They didn't know exactly where they were going, and they didn't know how long it would take, but Abram trusted God to take him to a land he could make his home.

God took them to the land of Canaan, a beautiful land good for growing food and grazing their flocks of sheep and goats. They passed by a holy place called Shechem, where there was a special tree called Moreh.

'This is the land that I am going to give to you and your people,' God told Abram.

Abram built an altar there to the Lord. He moved southwards to the hills near Bethel and pitched his tents there to make it his home.

WHICH PATH LEADS BACK TO THE TENT?

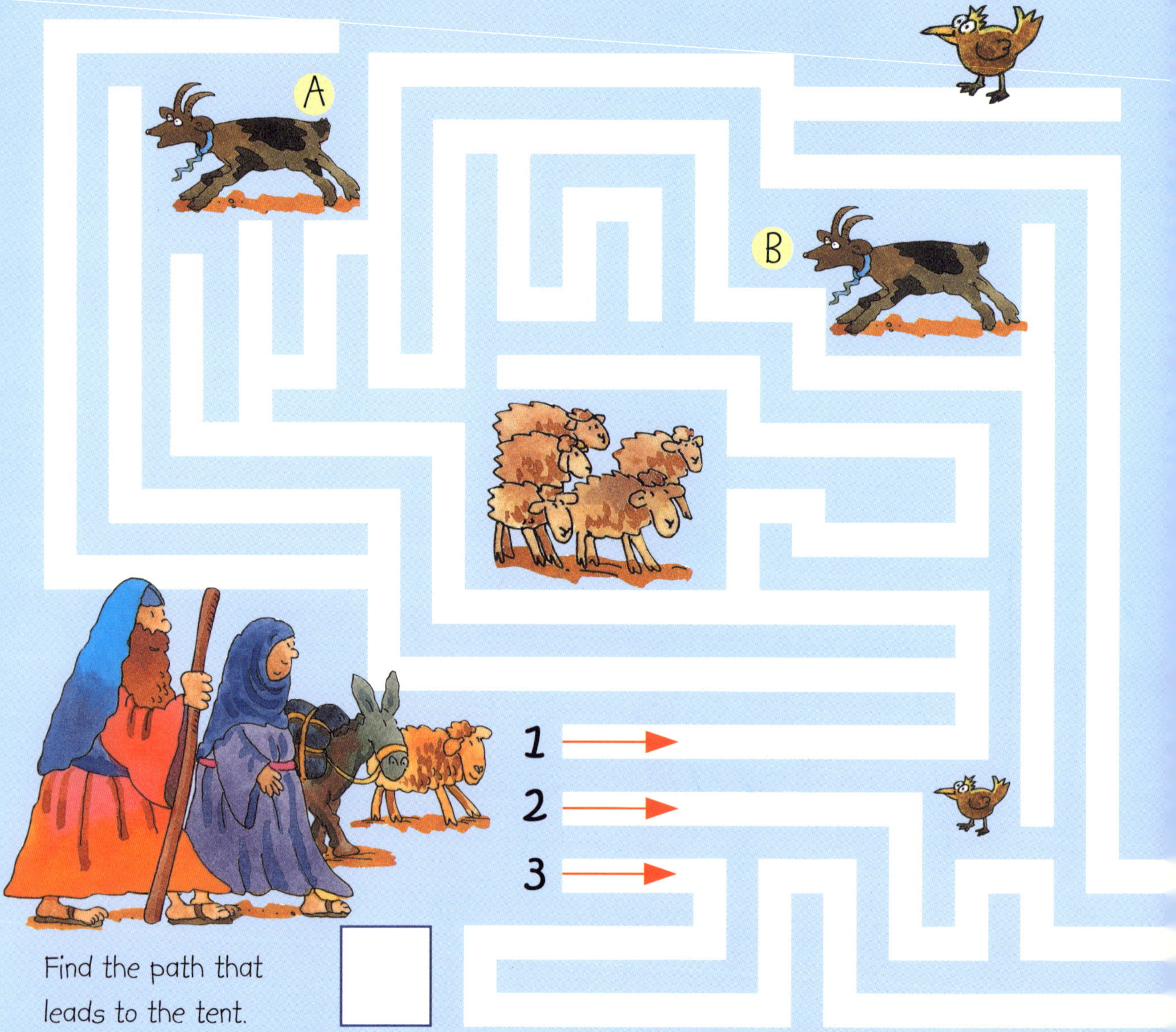

Find the path that leads to the tent.

IDENTICAL GOATS

Which two goats are identical twins?

A GIFT FROM GOD

Abram believed God's promise to bless him, but Abram and his wife Sarai still had no children.

'Look at the stars, and try to count them!' God said to Abram. 'You will have as many descendants as there are stars in the sky.'

God changed Abram's name to Abraham and Sarai's name to Sarah as a sign that God would give them a son.

One day, Abraham looked up and saw three men standing in front of him. 'Let me bring you some water!' said Abraham. 'Come and rest here a while. I will bring some food for you.'

Abraham hurried off to find Sarah.

'Quick! We have visitors!' he said. 'Bake some bread!' Then Abraham ran to find the best calf in his herd and told a servant to prepare it. He took the food and served it to his visitors.

'Where is your wife Sarah?' asked one of the men.

'She is still in the tent,' said Abraham.

'Nine months from now she will be nursing your son,' said the visitor.

Sarah laughed to herself. 'I am far too old for that!' she whispered.

But God was listening and said to Abraham, 'Is anything too hard for Me? Sarah will indeed have a son.'

Sure enough, nine months later, Sarah gave birth to baby Isaac.

Isaac brought great joy to his parents. He was a true gift from God.

Isaac grew up and married a beautiful girl called Rebecca. They had twin boys, Jacob and Esau. Abraham was their proud grandfather! God had kept His promise.

Sorting Abraham's Flock

Abraham and his family had many sheep and goats. Sort out the flock by putting **S** under each sheep and **G** under each goat.

Which animal is the odd one out? Put a cross under it.

What's hidden in the stars?

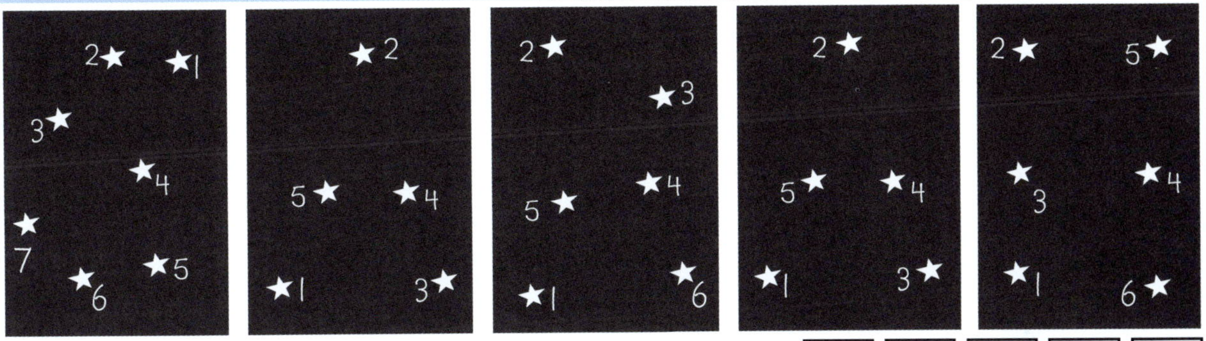

Connect the stars in the right order to find the answer.

Word puzzle

Unscramble the following words, then place them in the correct order in the grid. The unshaded letters will reveal the name of someone from the story.

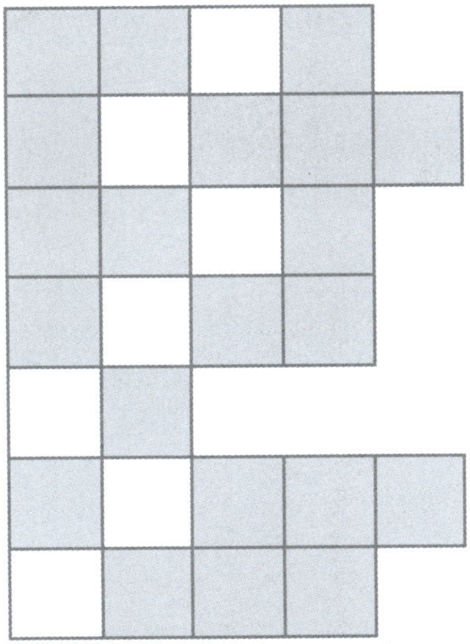

1) RATS
2) MR BAA
3) ROME
4) RACE
5) EH
6) MEANS
7) DAME

JACOB PLAYS A TRICK

Isaac's twin boys, Esau and Jacob, were quite a handful!

Even when they were inside their mum's tummy, they had jumped about and struggled against each other!

Esau had been born first. He was red and hairy all over. He grew up to love hunting and being outdoors. Jacob was born second, and came out holding tightly to his brother's heel! Jacob had smooth skin. He liked staying at home with his mother, Rebecca.

Esau was his father's favourite. One day, Esau would get his father's special blessing and all his riches. Jacob was his mother's special son.

One day, Esau came in from hunting and was very hungry. 'Give me some of that soup!' he asked his brother, Jacob.

Jacob had a cunning plan. 'Only if you give me your rights as the first-born son!'

'Oh all right, just give me some soup!' said Esau. Jacob smiled a cunning smile.

He was now going to be the one to get all his father's riches one day.

Father Isaac grew old and blind. One day he called for his son, Esau.

'My son, Esau, I am old. I might die one day soon. Go hunting and cook me some of that tasty food I like. Then I will give you my final blessing.'

Rebecca was listening at the door. She was going to help Jacob play a cruel

trick on his brother and father so that he would get the blessing instead.

She cooked Isaac's favourite dinner, put Esau's clothes on Jacob, then tied goatskin on to Jacob's arms to make them feel hairy.

Jacob went to his father with the soup. Isaac was tricked and thought it was Esau! So he gave him his special blessing.

Suddenly Esau came back from hunting, with a tasty meal for his father.

'Who are you?' asked Isaac.

'Your son, Esau!' replied the hairy son.

'I have been tricked!' trembled Isaac. 'Jacob has taken your blessing!'

Jacob ran away to live with his uncle Laban, as far away from angry Esau as he could go!

FAMILY TREE

This is the family tree of Noah and his sons. Can you fill in the missing names?

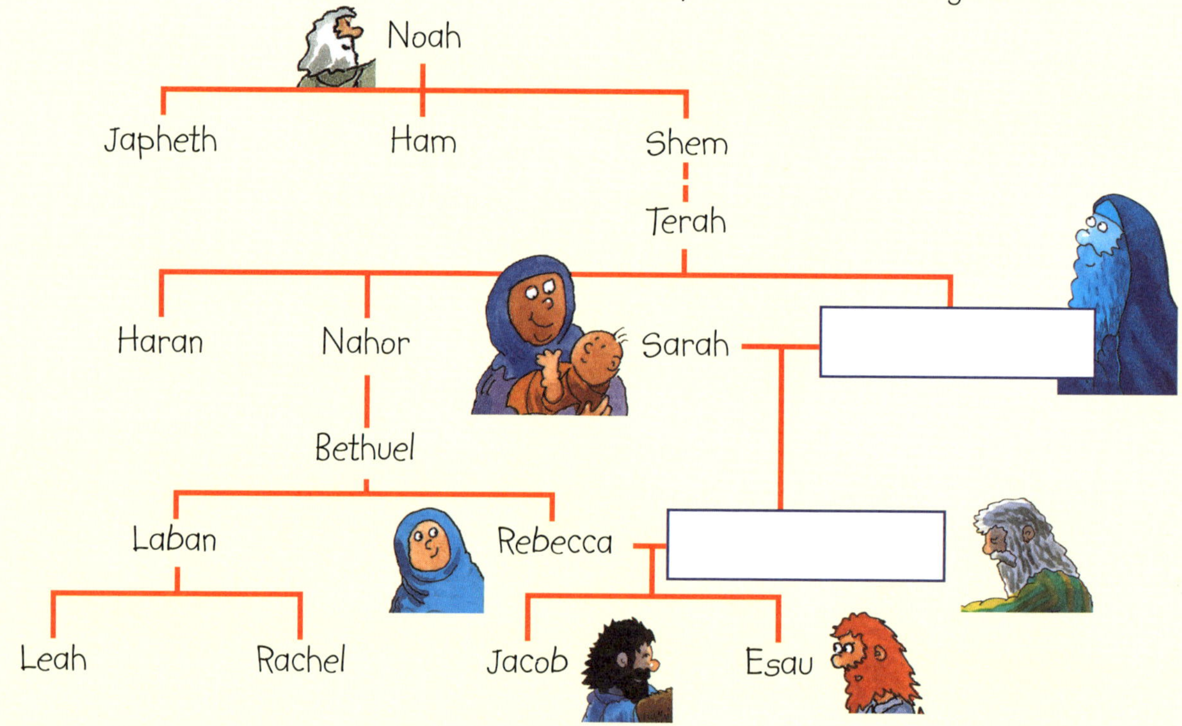

Who was Jacob's father?

Who was Esau's brother?

Who was Isaac's wife?

Who were Abraham's grandsons?

WHAT'S MISSING?

Put a circle around the part of each picture that is missing in each of the hunters below.

WHAT'S WRONG?

Look carefully at the picture. There are nine things that look wrong. Can you put a circle around each one?

JOSEPH'S JEALOUS BROTHERS

Jacob got married and had many children: twelve sons and one daughter.

Jacob also had a very large flock of sheep and goats.

Jacob loved all his children, but one was his favourite: Joseph. He was very special and Jacob loved him more than any of the others. This made Joseph feel pleased, but it made the other brothers feel very jealous indeed!

One day, Jacob gave Joseph a fabulous coat to wear. Joseph put it on and strutted up and down, showing his brothers how fine he looked in his new coat.

'Where's our coat?' they muttered. 'Why does Dad love him more than us?' They grew very angry.

One night Joseph had a strange dream. He told his brothers all about it the next day. But they didn't like what they heard!

'I dreamed we were all in the fields, gathering corn. Suddenly your sheaves of corn all made a circle around my sheaf of corn and bowed down to it!'

'Do you think you will rule over us?' sniggered the brothers. They hated Joseph. They were fed up.

To make matters worse, Joseph had another strange dream. Again, he told his brothers all about it:

'I dreamed I saw the sun and moon and eleven stars, all bowing down to me!'

'Not again!' said his brothers. 'Who does he think he is?! Does he think that his whole family will bow down to him now?'

The brothers were so angry they wanted to get rid of Joseph. They waited for the right moment ...

Any Questions?

The answers to the questions below can be found in the story on pages 38-39.

Q. How many sons did Jacob have?

Q How many daughters did Jacob have?

Q. Who was Jacob's favourite son?

Q. What did Jacob give to Joseph?

Q. Did Jacob give presents to his other sons?

Q. How did the brothers feel?

Q. What bowed down to Joseph in his first dream?

Q. Did Joseph dream again?

Q. How many stars did Joseph dream about?

Q. How did Joseph's brothers feel about him?

WHAT'S THIS?

Animals were very important to the families such as Jacob's. Find three **sheep** and three **goats** by crossing out the letters below. Which animal is left?

S T S S T S S G

C L E

A H P A H M P H O P

A

E G E G E T S

E O E E O A

CAN YOU DRAW?

Can you complete the picture of a sheep?

A SLAVE IN EGYPT

Joseph's brothers had a plan to get rid of their brother once and for all. They were fed up with all his boasting.

One day, when they were looking after the sheep in the fields, Joseph came up to them.

Joseph's brothers had seen him coming. 'Here comes the dreamer!' they sniggered. 'Let's kill him and throw him into a dry well. We'll tell Dad that a wild animal killed him. He'll never know.'

But Reuben liked Joseph.

'No, let's not kill him,' said Reuben. 'Let's just throw him in the well.'

Reuben secretly planned to rescue Joseph later and take him home.

Joseph arrived in the fields.

'How's it going?' asked Joseph.

Suddenly, the brothers grabbed Joseph, ripped off his fine coat and threw him into the well.

'Help!' shouted Joseph. 'What are you doing to me?!'

The brothers did not explain. They sat down to eat their lunch. Then some of the brothers saw a group of traders, on their way to Egypt with camels. 'Let's sell him to the traders!' said the brothers.

So Joseph was sold to be a slave and taken to Egypt.

The brothers had twenty pieces of silver in return.

They killed a goat and dipped Joseph's torn coat in the blood. They went to their father, Jacob, and told him the bad news. They didn't tell him the truth.

'A wild animal has killed Joseph!' wailed Jacob. 'My son is dead!'

Meanwhile, Joseph was sold to a man named Potiphar, one of the King's officers.

Many years later, the brothers went to Egypt looking for food. They didn't expect to see Joseph again. But Joseph had done well for himself in Egypt. He was now in favour with the King and had a gold chain around his neck!

Joseph tested his brothers and knew that they were sorry for what they had done to him all those years ago. Joseph forgave them, hugged them and was reunited with his father. Jacob was overjoyed to find his son alive again.

SPOT THE MISTAKE!

WHO DID IT?

Which two brothers dipped the coat in the blood?

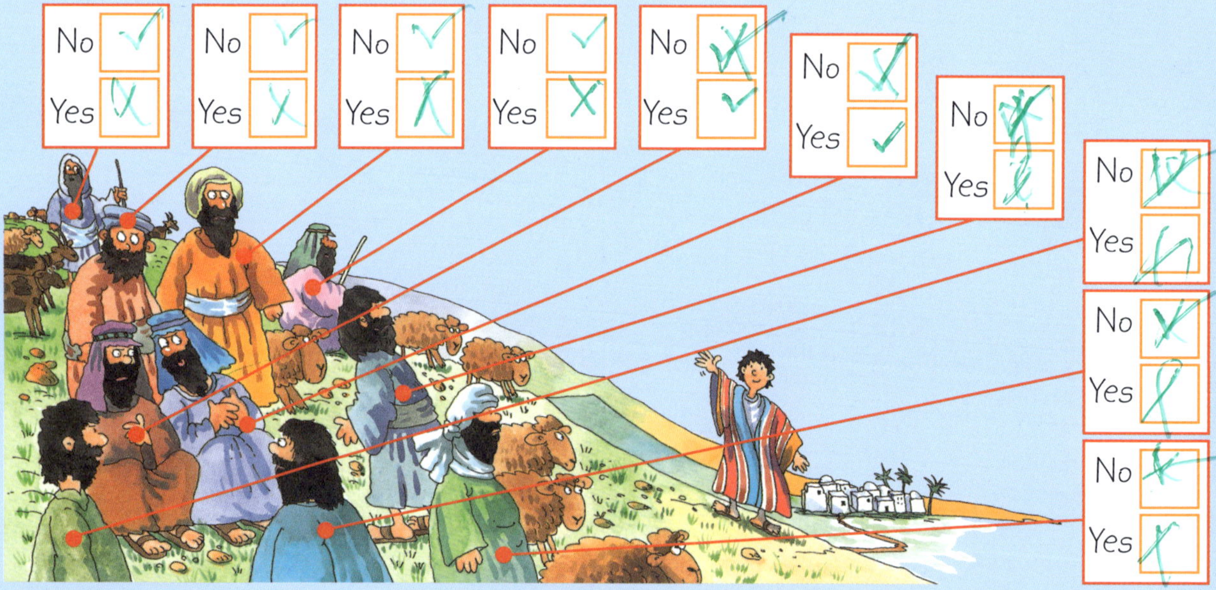

Put a circle around each of the five mistakes in the picture above.

CAN YOU SPOT THE REAL JOSEPH?

Which Joseph matches the real Joseph pictured in the box? Circle the number.

THE BABY IN THE BASKET

Many years had passed since Joseph lived in Egypt. There was a new cruel king on the throne now. He turned the Israelite people into his slaves. He made them work all day in the baking sun.

The king was afraid that the slaves might turn against him so he commanded his soldiers to drown the newborn boys of each Israelite family in the River Nile!

One mother hid her baby for three months where the soldiers could not find him. When the baby started to grow too big for the hiding place, she made a special basket of reeds, painted it with tar to make it waterproof and put her baby in it. Lovingly she carried the basket down to the river and hid it in the reeds while the baby's sister, Miriam, watched from a distance.

When the king's daughter came down to the river to bathe, the princess heard the baby crying.

'An Israelite *baby*!' she cried.

Miriam stepped forward bravely. 'Shall I find someone to feed him?'

When the princess agreed, Miriam ran to fetch her own mother.

'Look after the baby for me until he is big enough to live in the palace,' said the princess. 'I will pay you.'

The baby was called Moses. He grew big and strong and lived in the royal palace.

WORDSEARCH

There are twelve words hidden in the grid, all of which appear in the story. Cross each one out and write it alongside the grid. The words may be written in any direction.

M	S	E	V	A	L	S	H	B	P
I	O	R	K	E	D	E	O	A	P
R	V	S	C	E	F	Y	L	J	R
I	G	T	E	K	S	A	B	I	I
A	U			S	C			T	N
M	R			E	Y			E	C
O	G			H	B			L	E
T	L			T	A			P	S
H	B			A	B			O	S
E	D			B	M			E	L
R	B			C	D			P	F

IT'S A BABY!

Can you complete the picture?

CREEPY BUGS

Can you spot the ten beetles hiding in the picture?

LET MY PEOPLE GO

'Moses! Moses!' came God's voice. 'I have seen how cruel the ruler of Egypt is to My people. I have heard the slaves crying. I will bring them out of Egypt and take them to a land of their own. Go to the king of Egypt. Tell him to let My people go!'

Moses was astonished.

'But I am nobody special!' said Moses. 'Why should the king listen to me?'

'I will be with you,' said God. 'Now go!'

So Moses and his brother Aaron went to the king of Egypt.

'The Lord, the God of Israel, says you must let His people go!' said Moses.

The King of Egypt laughed.

'No, I will not let my slaves go!'

'Then disasters will strike Egypt,' said Moses.

Moses went down to the River Nile and put his stick in the water. The water turned to blood. All the fish died. But the king refused to listen to Moses.

God sent a plague of frogs. They hopped into the houses and into the

kitchens. Then came a gigantic swarm of gnats and then flies to bite the Egyptians.

Next came a terrible disease that killed the animals in the fields. Horses, donkeys, cows, sheep and goats lay dead on the ground.

People found terrible boils on their skin. Hailstones pelted the land. Locusts ate all the crops. But still the King would not listen to Moses.

So God sent darkness to cover the land. Then every single firstborn son of Egypt died. The King of Egypt sent for Moses. 'Get out of my land!' he wailed. 'And take your people. I will let them go.'

Moses led the Israelite people out of Egypt.

MISSING VOWELS

Replace all the vowels - a, e, i, o, u - that have been left out of the part of the story written below, so the story reads correctly.

_N_ D_Y G_D S_ _D T_ M_S_S

'MY P_ _PL_ _R_ _NH_PPY.

_ W_NT Y_ _ T_ T_LL TH_

K_NG _F _GYPT T_ L_T TH_M G_'.

TRUE OF FALSE?

Tick the box which shows whether these pictures were among the ten plagues.

TRUE ☐
FALSE ☐

TRUE ☐
FALSE ☐

TRUE ☐
FALSE ☐

TRUE ☐
FALSE ☐

HIDDEN ANSWERS

Can you answer the questions using the words hidden in the box?

1) Who were slaves in Egypt?

2) What was the name of the river?

3) What colour did the river turn?

4) Which creature ate the crops?

5) Who was Moses scared of?

6) What fell from the sky?

7) Which creatures got sick?

8) What could people not leave?

9) Which plague came in swarms?

10) Which green creatures were in the food?

I	J	K	L	I	A	H
S	S	G	O	R	F	V
R	W	A	T	C	H	W
A	O	D	H	F	O	P
E	C	S	E	G	U	H
L	L	E	K	B	S	R
I	R	I	I	C	E	F
T	Y	L	N	D	S	H
E	T	F	G	Y	K	I
S	T	S	U	C	O	L

TRUE ☐
FALSE ☐

TRUE ☐
FALSE ☐

TRUE ☐
FALSE ☐

TRUE ☐
FALSE ☐

THE GREAT ESCAPE

God led His people out of Egypt through the desert and towards the Red Sea. During the day, God went in front of them in a pillar of cloud to show the way. During the night, God went in front of them in a pillar of fire to give them light.

They camped near the Red Sea.

But it wasn't long before the king of Egypt changed his mind.

'What have I done?!' he shouted. 'Now I have lost all my slaves! I must get those people back here to work for me!'

So the king sent his soldiers after the Israelites!

He got his war chariot ready and his army. There were six hundred of the finest chariots in Egypt, horses and drivers and many more soldiers besides.

The Israelites were trapped by the Red Sea.

'What can we do now?' they wailed to Moses. 'If we turn back, we will be captured by the king. If we go forwards, we will surely drown in the Red Sea! Moses, why did you bring us here to die? Why didn't you leave us alone where we were? It is better to be a slave than to die in the desert!'

'Don't be afraid!' replied Moses. 'You will see what God will do to save you today. The Lord will fight for you.'

God had a plan. He told Moses to lift his stick and hold it over the waters of the sea. The water divided and the Israelites were able to walk across on the dry land!

As soon as they had crossed the Red Sea, Moses held out his stick again. God sent a powerful wind to close up the waters of the sea. All the Egyptians who had been chasing Moses and his people were washed away by the sea and drowned.

Moses and the Israelites sang a song of praise to God for rescuing them from the evil king of Egypt. They were on a journey to the promised land.

FRAGMENTS

Which of the fragments below fit into the six red shapes in the large picture?

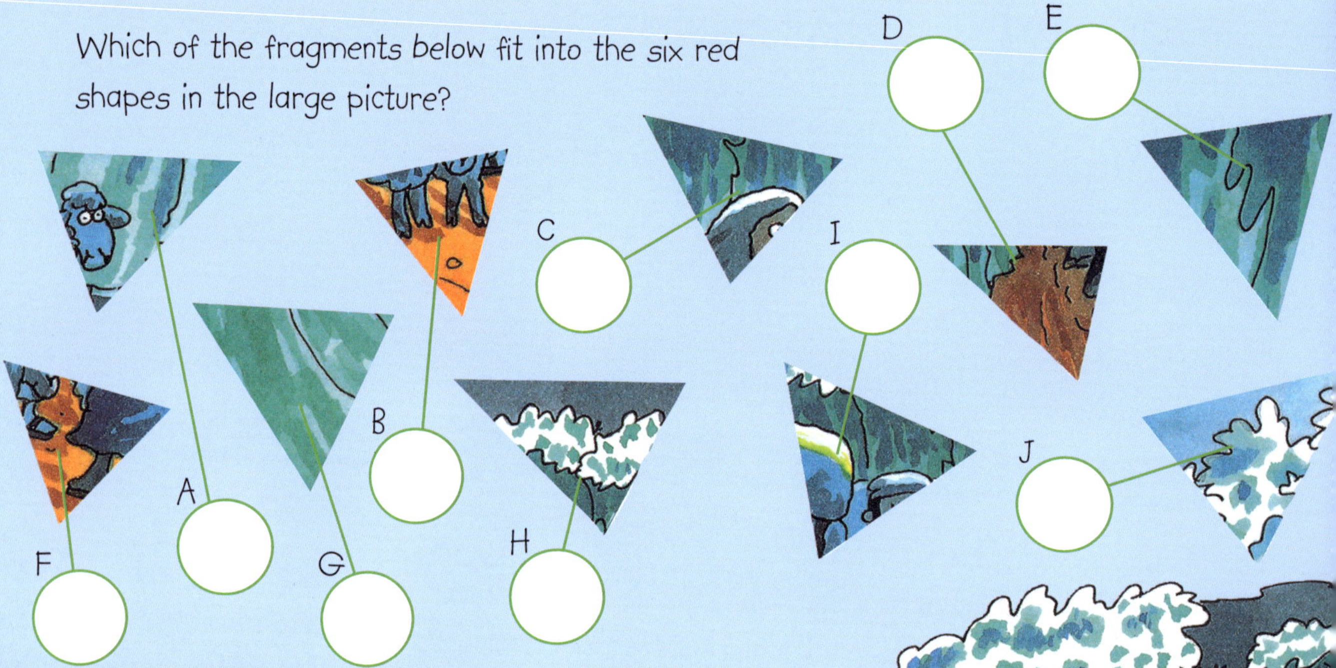

SOMETHING'S DIFFERENT

Can you find four differences in this detail taken from the larger picture opposite?

Spot the spelling mistakes

There are two spelling mistakes on each line. Can you find all ten mistakes?

'What can we doo now?' they wailed to Moses. 'If we turn bak, we will bea captured by the King. If we go forwerds, we will surely drown in the Red See! Moses, why did you bring us here to diy? Why didn't you leeve us alone where we were? It is beter to be a slave than to dye in the desart!'

JOSHUA AND THE BATTLE OF JERICHO

Joshua was chosen by God to be the next leader of his people.

'I will be with you, as I was with Moses,' said God. 'I will never leave you. Don't be afraid, for I, the Lord, am with you wherever you go.'

The Israelite people were still on their way to the promised land.

First the people had to pass through the city of Jericho. The stone walls of the city were very thick and impossible to get through. The gates were locked so the Israelites could not get into the city. Guards kept watch day and night.

Joshua believed God would help them. He listened to God's plan.

God told Joshua to choose seven priests who would carry trumpets made of rams' horns. They were to march around the city once every day for six days, blowing their trumpets in front of the people.

On the seventh day, the priests would march round the city six times. On the seventh time, the priests would sound a long, loud note on their rams' horns, and the people would give a great shout.

So that is exactly what Joshua and the people did. They marched round the city each day until, on the seventh day and on the seventh march, the people gave a great shout.

The walls of the city collapsed!

Joshua and his people captured the city. Joshua always listened to God's words and was careful to obey God's laws.

When he was a very old man, he told the Israelites to keep on serving God.

'As for me and my family,' said Joshua, 'we will always serve the Lord.'

WORD PUZZLE

Look carefully at the grid of letters. Only one row contains the correct spelling of one word JERICHO. Which row is it?

1	J	E	R	I	R	E	E
2	J	E	E	I	I	O	H
3	J	E	R	I	H	O	I
4	J	E	R	I	C	H	O
5	J	E	R	J	I	O	I
6	J	E	R	I	H	O	C
7	J	E	R	I	I	H	C

WORD JUMBLE

The following sentences and parts of sentences have all been taken from the story 'Joshua and the Battle of Jericho' but they don't make sense because the words are jumbled up. Without looking at the story, can you write the sentence correctly underneath?

Leave never will I you.

____

to get impossible through. and thick

____

Kept night. watch Guards day and

____

plan. listened God's to He

____

of collapsed! walls the city The

____

the always Lord. serve we will

____

Picture Puzzle

If you look carefully at the piles of rocks surrounding the city of Jericho you will find letters that, when put together, reveal some of the people mentioned in the story. Write them here.

Late Starter?

Can you spot the odd one out?

1 2 3 4 5 6 7

SAMUEL'S SLEEPLESS NIGHT

Hannah had longed for a child for many years. She prayed for a child of her own. God heard her prayers and blessed her with a son. She called him Samuel.

Hannah wanted Samuel to serve God in the temple at Shiloh as a way of thanking God for her son. So Samuel lived far away from his parents' home.

He helped Eli the priest, who was a very old man. Eli loved God and served Him. But Eli's sons did not follow God's laws.

One night, when Eli was asleep, Samuel heard a voice calling his name.

'Samuel! Samuel!'

'Yes, here I am,' said Samuel, running into Eli's room. He thought it was Eli who had called him.

'I did not call you. Go back to bed, Samuel,' said Eli. So Samuel went back to bed. The voice called again: 'Samuel! Samuel!'

Again, Samuel ran to Eli. 'Here I am!' he said.

'I didn't call,' said Eli. 'Go back to bed, Samuel!' Again Samuel settled back down

in his bed. But not for long.

'Samuel! Samuel!'

came the voice. He ran to Eli.

This time, Eli realised who was calling. It was the voice of God.

'If He calls again, say, "Speak, Lord, Your servant is listening." '

So Samuel went back to bed. This time he was ready.

'Samuel! Samuel!' came the voice.

'Speak, Lord, Your servant is listening,' said Samuel.

And God spoke to Samuel. In the morning, Samuel told Eli all that God had said. God was going to punish Eli's sons for the bad things they were doing.

Everything he said came true.

WORD PUZZLE

How much can you remember from the story? The answers to the questions can all be found in the grid by going across one row, then back along the next. When you have all the answers, which words have been mentioned more than twice?

1 A	B	A	B	Y	2 G	O	D	3 A	B
L	E 5	L	E	U	M	A	S 4	Y	O
I	T	H	E	P	R	I	E	S	T
E	L	P	M	E	T	S	D	O	G 6
7 A	V	O	I	C	E	8 S	A	M	U
M	O	O	R	S	I	L	E 9	L	E
10 T	H	R	E	E	11 G	O	D	12 S	A
L	E	U	M	A	S	L	E	U	M

1) What did Hannah pray for? ____________________

2) Who answered Hannah's prayer? ____________________

3) What gift did God give Hannah? ____________________

4) What was the boy called? ____________________

5) Who taught the boy about God? ____________________

6) Where did Eli take the boy to live? ____________________

7) What woke the boy up when he was sleeping? ____________________

8) What was said? ____________________

9) Where did the boy run to when he heard the voice? ____________________

10) How many times did Samuel run into Eli's room? ____________________

11) Who wanted to speak with Samuel? ____________________

12) What did the voice say? ____________________

Which answers are mentioned more than twice? ____________________

Picture Puzzle

There are five differences between these two pictures. Draw a circle around each of them.

THE SHEPHERD BOY

David was a handsome young man. He took care of his father Jesse's sheep and could scare away wild animals that came near. He could play the harp and sing very well.

The prophet Samuel was sent by God to choose one of Jesse's sons to be the next King. Samuel was worried and asked God, 'What if the present King, Saul, hears about this! He will be very angry and might even kill me!'

But God told Samuel to go to visit Jesse's family.

One of Jesse's sons was very tall and handsome, but this was not the man God wanted to be King. Jesse brought seven of his sons to Samuel, but none of them was the one God had chosen.

Samuel asked, 'Have you any more sons?'

'Only the youngest,' replied Jesse. 'He is out looking after the sheep.'

They sent for him to come and see Samuel. God said to Samuel, 'This is the one. Anoint him!'

So Samuel took some olive oil and

anointed David in front of all the brothers. From that day on, God's spirit was with David.

The present King was called Saul. He was a troubled man. He didn't always do as God wanted and this made him fearful. An evil spirit came upon him and made him feel terrible.

'I need someone to play the harp to me!' said King Saul.

One of the King's servants told Saul about David. 'David is a brave and handsome man, a good soldier and he plays the harp well.'

'Bring him to me,' said King Saul.

So David came to play his harp for Saul. Whenever the evil spirit came upon the king, David played beautiful music. The spirit left him and Saul felt much better again.

King Saul didn't know that David had been anointed to be the next King of Israel.

SPOT THE DIFFERENCES

There are eight differences between these pictures. Make a circle around each of them.

WORD PUZZLE

WAS	SHEPHERD
SAID	SAMUEL
ISRAEL	DAVID
STEAL	SHEEP
LAMBS	JESSE
GOD	SEVEN
BEARS	SPIRIT
WHAT	HANDSOME
BUT	STRONG
ARRIVED	KING

L	L	L	E	U	M	A	S	H
S	A	I	D	J	I	K	A	B
R	E	M	T	Y	I	N	R	G
D	T	U	B	N	D	J	R	N
R	S	M	G	S	E	N	I	O
E	R	X	O	S	T	V	V	R
H	A	M	S	I	D	P	E	T
P	E	E	R	I	D	E	D	S
E	B	I	V	O	G	E	F	A
H	P	A	G	T	A	H	W	W
S	D	L	E	A	R	S	I	F

All these words can be found hidden in the grid. They may go up, down, across, diagonally or even backwards. Can you find all the words in the grid?

COUNT THE CROWNS

How many crowns can you find hidden in the picture?

Answer ________

DAVID AND THE GIANT

King Saul's army was fighting the Philistines. It was always fighting the Philistines! Three of David's brothers were in the army.

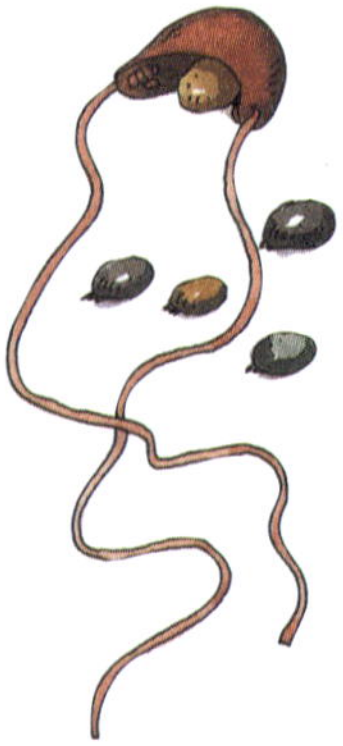

One day, their father sent David to the army camp with some food to give to his brothers.

As he came near to the army camp, David heard a booming voice. It came from a giant of a man! It was Goliath, the Philistine champion.

King Saul had promised a big reward to the man who could kill Goliath. But no one dared to try!

'No one should be afraid of this man! He is not just challenging us. He is challenging God Himself!' said David. 'I will fight him! God has saved me from the lion and the bear when I have been looking after my sheep. God will save me now.'

David tried on the King's armour, but it was far too big. He decided to meet the giant without it. David went to the brook with his sling, picked up five smooth stones and put them in his bag.

When Goliath saw David, he laughed a cruel laugh.

'You have a sword and a spear,' said David, 'but I have God on my side!'

David took a stone out of his bag, put it in his sling, whizzed it round his head and fired it at the giant. The stone hit Goliath in the middle of his forehead and he fell to the ground with a mighty crash!

David grabbed Goliath's sword and chopped off his head.

When the Philistines saw that their hero was dead, they ran away as fast as they could! God had given David the victory. All the people cheered for him.

Spot the Difference

Can you spot ten differences in the two pictures? Put a circle round them.

Anagrams

Unscramble these words from the story on pages 70-71.

TAG IN

RIDE LOSS

TEN SOS

HARPS

DID AV

WORDS

CEDARS

R PEAS

SHED OUT

LINGS

Crossword

Can you fit the following words into their correct places?
It helps if you start with the longest word.

3 See
Die
Did
Big
4 Went
Food
Legs
Army
5 Sharp
Sling
Giant
6 Stones
Strong
Roared
Living
7 Goliath

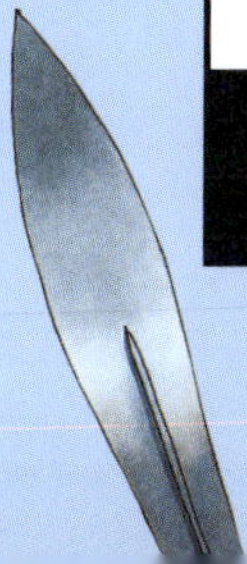

GOD TAKES CARE OF ELIJAH

Elijah had been called by God to be a prophet. He gave messages from God to the people of Israel and their King.

One day Elijah went to see King Ahab. Ahab did not care about following God's ways and his wife was even worse. She worshipped the false god, Baal.

Elijah warned the King to listen to God but Ahab and his wife refused to listen.

'Then I must tell you this,' said Elijah. 'There will be no rain for the next two or three years until God sends it!'

Now Elijah's life was in danger. God told him to go east and hide near the brook in the Kerith Ravine.

God looked after Elijah. He ordered ravens to bring him bread and meat every morning and every evening. And Elijah drank the water in the brook of the ravine until it dried up.

Then God told Elijah to go to a town called Zarephath, where a widow would help him.

Elijah saw a woman gathering firewood. 'Please bring me a drink of water,' Elijah said to her. 'And some bread, too, please.'

The widow and her son were nearly starving, as all her food was running out. During the drought there was no rain to water the crops. But she kindly offered to make a small loaf of bread for Elijah with the little bit of flour and oil she had left.

'Don't worry,' said Elijah. 'You won't starve. God says the jar of flour and this jug of oil will never be empty until the day it rains again,' said Elijah.

Sure enough, there was always enough flour and oil in the jar to feed them all! God looked after Elijah.

BUILD THE PICTURE

Re-create this picture by putting the squares in the right place.
Write the number of the correct position in each circle.

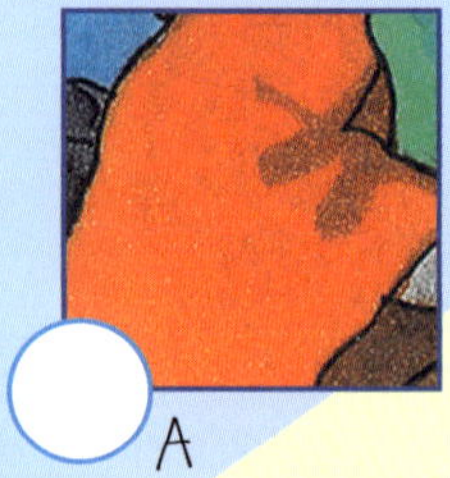
A

B

C

D

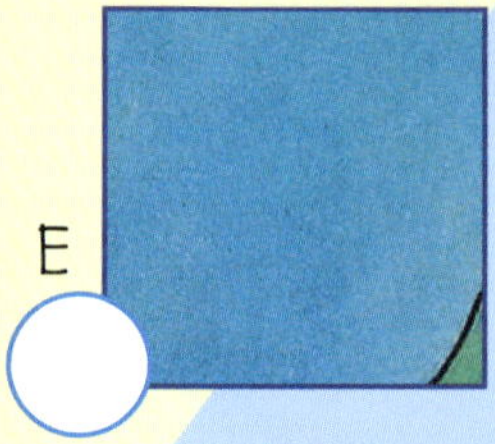
E

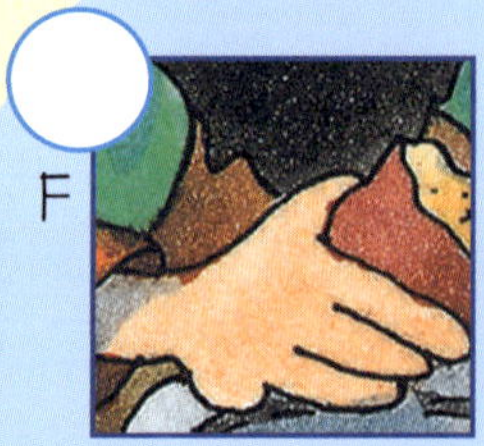
F

G

H

I

1	2	3
4	5	6
7	8	9

STORY QUIZ

Write the answers to the questions in the boxes below.

What is the name for a long period without rain?

What kind of bird did God send to feed Elijah?

What did God call Elijah to be?

What did the widow offer to make?

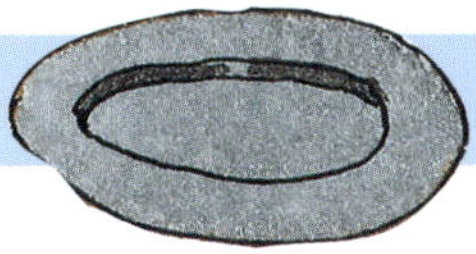

What false God did king Ahab's wife worship?

What was the widow collecting when she met Elijah?

Name one of the things that never ran out?

FIRE FROM HEAVEN

It was nearly three years since Elijah had seen King Ahab. The land was dry and parched. Now God told Elijah to return to see the king again.

Elijah was not afraid. He gave the king God's message as he had done before.

'You have turned away from the true God and worshipped Baal instead. Now we will have a contest to see who is the one true God. The people must choose whom they will worship. Ask the prophets of Baal to come to Mount Carmel.'

When the hundreds of prophets who worshipped Baal had gathered on the mountain, Elijah spoke to them all.

'The prophets of Baal will put one bull on their altar. I will put another bull on the altar of the Lord. The Baal worshippers will call on Baal to burn up their bull. I will call on the one true God to burn up the other

bull. We will see who answers!'

The prophets of Baal shouted all day, but no fire came.

'Shout louder!' said Elijah. 'Maybe he is daydreaming, or on the toilet! Or maybe he has gone on a journey! He might be asleep and you'll have to wake him up!'

There was still no answer from Baal.

Next it was Elijah's turn. Elijah asked his servants to pour water on the altar three times. It ran down the altar and filled a trench around the altar.

Elijah prayed loudly, 'Answer my prayer, O God. Show these people that You are

the true God of Israel! Show these people that You are God and that You are bringing them back to Yourself!'

God answered Elijah's prayer. He sent down fire from heaven. It burnt up the bull, the wood and the stones, and dried up all the water in the trench!

The people watching were amazed and shouted, 'The Lord is God!'

The prophets of Baal tried to run away but Elijah did not let them escape.

Then clouds began to appear in the sky. The drought was ended. God was sending rain again to water the land.

MAKE FIRE!

Copy the fire illustration into the grid opposite.

MATHS

THREE WHAT?

HUNDREDS OF WHAT?

PROPHETS

ONE WHAT?

The answers are in the story on pages 78-79.

PAIRS

A

B

These men all look the same but they are not! Draw a line between each pair of men that match each other.

C

D

E

F

G

H

NAAMAN AND THE LITTLE SERVANT GIRL

Naaman had won many battles and was a very important general in the Syrian army. One day, Naaman's army took a little girl from Israel to be a servant in Naaman's household. The girl worked hard and liked her master and mistress.

Naaman fell ill with a terrible disease. It was leprosy. His skin turned white and sore and no one could cure him.

The little girl in Naaman's household said to her mistress one day, 'I wish that my master would go and see Elisha, the prophet in Samaria! I am sure he could heal Naaman of this disease!'

Naaman had nothing to lose. He got permission to go and took a letter and gifts to King Joram.

The king was horrified when Naaman arrived in Samaria with his horses and chariots. He didn't know how he could help the commander. But Elisha told the king to send Naaman to him so that he could show him that there was a God in Israel who could heal people.

When Naaman arrived at the prophet's house, he expected to be welcomed in. But Elisha would not see Naaman. Instead he

just sent a message to him.

'Go and wash seven times in the River Jordan. Then you will be healed!'

Naaman was angry. He thought Elisha would at least come out and pray for him.

'Just try it and see,' said Naaman's servants. 'If he had asked you to do something difficult, you would have done it!'

So Naaman went down to the river and dipped himself in it seven times. To his amazement, he was completely healed. His white, wrinkled skin became as soft and pink as a baby's skin!

Naaman returned to Elisha and said, 'Now I know that there is no other god but the God of Israel.'

Naaman returned home, amazed at what God had done for him.

FRAGMENTS

Which of the fragments below fit into the six yellow shapes in the large picture?

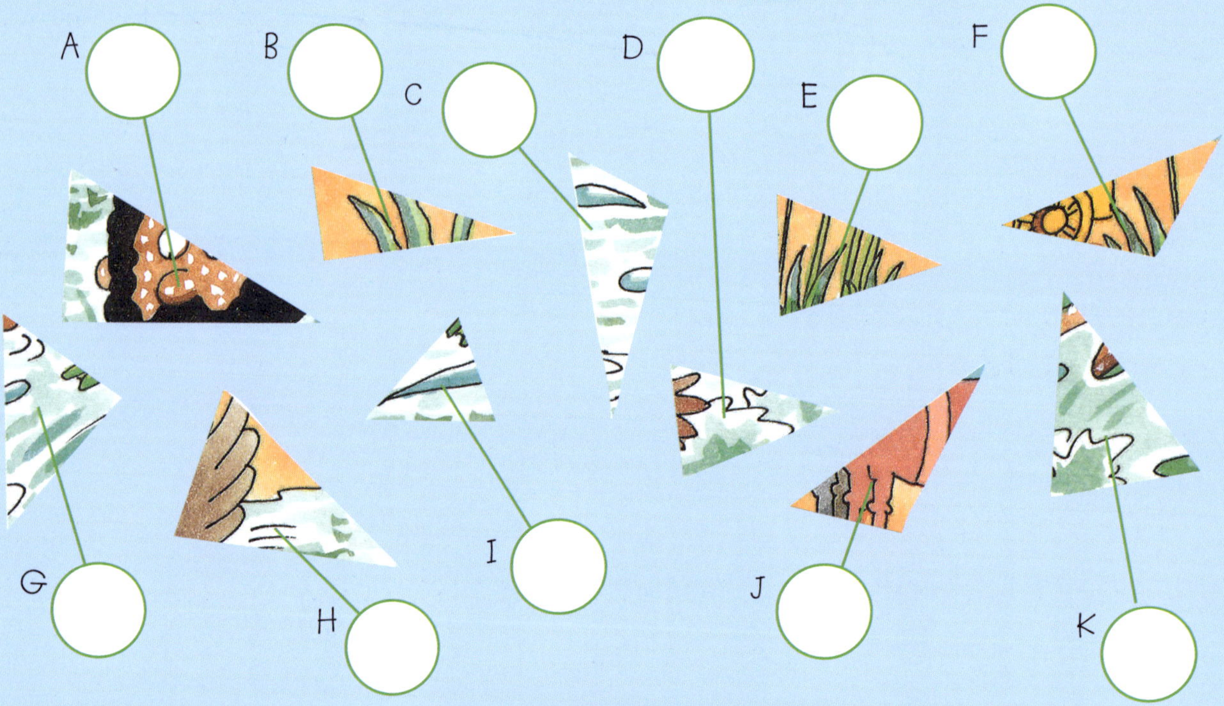

EDIT THE TEXT

Can you find six mistakes in the following extract from the story?

'Go and wish six times in the River Thames. Then you will be healed!'

Naaaman was happy. He thought Moses would at least come out and pray for him.

DANIEL IN THE LIONS' DEN

Daniel loved God and wanted to serve Him wherever he went.

One day, he was taken captive by a foreign king and made to serve in the king's court. Daniel was certain that he would always serve God, even if it got him into trouble.

Daniel worked hard and became an important leader in the king's court. But some men were very jealous of him. They tried to get him into trouble.

The king had made a rule that, for

thirty days, everyone in the land must worship no one but the King. Anyone found worshipping someone else must be thrown to the lions!

Of course, Daniel continued to worship God. So the jealous men arrested Daniel and took him to be fed to the hungry lions!

The King was very upset. He felt he had been tricked into making the rule about worshipping only the King. But now there was no choice. He had to let Daniel be thrown to the lions.

'May your God rescue you!' said the King.

It was a long night for the King. He waited to see what had happened to Daniel. He feared the worst.

At last, morning came, and the King ran to the lions' den.

'Daniel! Are you alive?' he called. He didn't expect to hear a reply.

'Yes, I'm alive!' shouted Daniel. 'God sent an angel to shut the mouths of the lions. They did not hurt me.'

The King was so happy to see Daniel again. He was angry with the jealous men in his court and ordered that they be thrown to the lions instead!

Daniel was free and could pray to God wherever he liked.

WORD SEARCH

WHO	BABYLON
GOD	KINGDOM
LIVED	HUNGRY
WRONG	DARIUS
DANIEL	THIRTY
ANGEL	KING
HONEST	LIONS
SHARP	DEN
WORSHIP	CLAWS
NOT	TEETH

B	L	O	A	S	N	O	I	L	K
W	A	I	S	H	A	R	P	I	C
O	K	B	V	Y	R	G	N	U	H
R	I	K	Y	E	C	G	W	L	T
S	N	O	T	L	D	R	E	S	E
H	G	H	A	O	O	G	E	U	E
I	V	W	M	N	N	N	B	I	T
P	S	S	G	A	O	N	F	R	H
Y	T	R	I	H	T	S	E	A	V
D	O	G	L	E	I	N	A	D	P

Written *above* are lots of words to do with the story of Daniel. Can you find all the words hidden in the grid? Remember, they may go up, down, across, diagonally or even *backwards*.

PICTURE PUZZLE

Cross out all the letters that appear more than once in the *bubble* and then unscramble the remaining letters to spell out a word from the story.

Answer ....

JOIN THE DOTS

Connect all the dots, starting with 1 and finishing at 82, to add another big lion to the den.

JONAH RUNS AWAY

'Go to Nineveh!' God said to Jonah. 'Speak to the people and tell them I know all the terrible things they are doing. Tell them they must stop! They must do good things and learn to be kind to each other – or I must destroy them!'

But Jonah ran away. He did not want to go to Nineveh and do as God asked. He was afraid. He ran in the opposite direction and boarded a ship with a crew ready to sail to Spain.

Jonah felt safe. He went below deck, settled down and fell asleep. He did not notice the storm that was brewing, or the waves lashing the ship. Jonah slept on.

God made the storm rock the ship violently. All the sailors feared for their lives. They threw their cargo overboard but still the storm raged on.

Then the sailors found that Jonah was sleeping. They woke him up and made him call on God.

'It's all my fault!' Jonah shouted above the roaring wind. 'I ran away from God. You must throw me into the sea and then you will be safe!'

The sailors did not want to harm Jonah but they realised there was nothing else they could do. They threw him overboard and at once the sea became calm.

The ship sailed away, leaving the sailors amazed at God's power.

Jonah sank down into the deep, cold, dark sea. He thought he would drown and called to God to help him.

God answered Jonah's prayer. A huge fish opened his mouth and took Jonah into his belly. There Jonah prayed to God and sang praises to Him.

After three days, the fish spat Jonah out on to a beach.

God asked Jonah again to go to Nineveh. This time Jonah obeyed.

Jonah told the people of Nineveh what God had said. They listened to God's message and were sorry when they realised all the wrong things they had done. They turned back to God and asked Him to forgive them.

God loved the people. He was no longer angry with them. They had listened, said sorry and changed their ways. Now God could forgive them.

Word search

For each of these questions there is a one-word answer hidden in the grid. Find the answers and write them next to the questions.

1) Was Jonah a prophet or a shepherd? ____________
2) Did God tell Jonah that the people in Nineveh were good or wicked? ____________
3) Did Jonah find a ship or a camel to help him run away? ____________
4) What happened to the ship in the storm: it went up and? ____________
5) Were the sailors brave or scared? ____________
6) Jonah sank down into the deep, cold, dark? ____________
7) What did God send to help save Jonah: a huge fish or a huge wave? ____________
8) Was Jonah swallowed or chewed? ____________
9) Did the people of Nineveh listen to or ignore God's message? ____________
10) Did God forgive or punish the people? ____________
11) In the storm, were the waves high or low? ____________

P	R	O	P	H	E	T
N	E	T	S	I	L	S
			J	H	E	F
			N	A	I	O
			H	S	A	P
		W	H	W		
		I	D	A		
		C	O	L		
		K	W	L		
		E	N	O		
		D	E	W		
		D	V	E		
		E	I	D		
		R	G	H		
		A	R	G		
		C	O	I		
		S	F	H		

What do the remaining letters spell?

Picture Puzzle

Look at the six pictures of poor Jonah being thrown overboard and see if you can put them in the correct order.

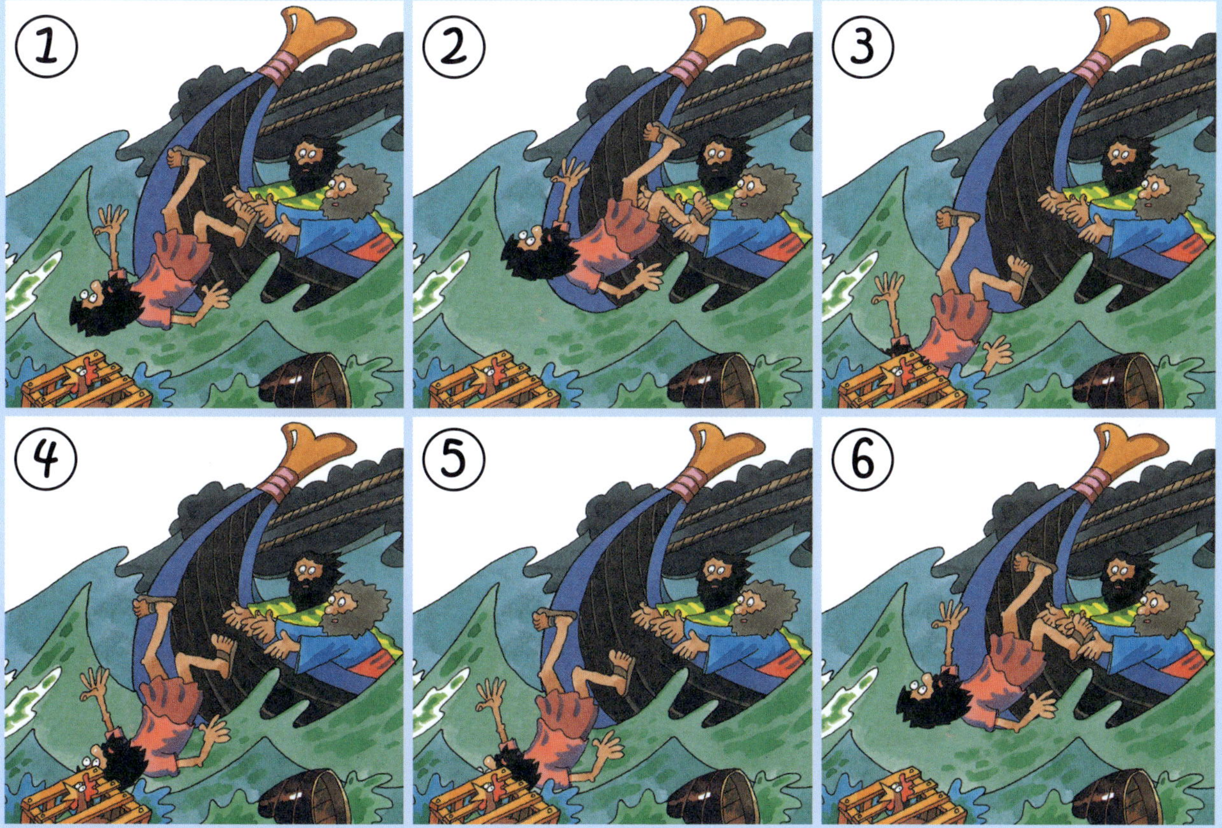

Answer ______ ______ ______ ______ ______ ______

Solutions to the Puzzles from the Old Testament

The Beautiful Garden
Pages 12-13

- The answers are circled.
- Happy - Sad,
  Dark - Light,
  Empty - Full,
  Love - Hate,
  Sand - Sea

S	U	P	L	A	N	T	S
O	K	P	J	K	N	E	D
E	B	Y	C	X	A	V	R
A	I	A	D	A	M	E	I
R	G	S	E	E	R	T	B
T	O	F	I	S	H	E	R
H	N	B	P	O	J	U	R
I	S	L	A	M	I	N	A

The Enemy in the Garden
Pages 16-17

- The answers are circled.
- There are three birds, nine animals, eleven pairs of eyes, eight trees and sixteen flowers in the garden.
- The answers are circled.

B	E	A	U	T	I	F	U	L	S
Y	G	J	E	B	V	C	D	S	E
G	U	P	O	V	B	T	R	T	L
C	A	D	A	M	E	N	I	I	B
K	M	R	L	M	E	E	B	U	A
O	Y	U	D	V	R	P	E	R	T
X	C	E	T	E	T	R	V	F	E
H	W	T	B	V	N	E	D	O	G
A	N	I	M	A	L	S	K	I	E
B	E	B	W	O	P	L	J	H	V

The Triple-Decker Boat
Pages 20-21

- This is a **lion**.
  This is a **cow**.
  This is a **goat**.
  These are **monkeys**.
  This is an **ostrich**.
- The answers are circled in the grid.

G	O	D	H	O	P	K
V	A	B	X	M	I	T
E	F	R	N	C	Z	P
R	A	C	D	N	E	X
T	M	A	D	E	W	J
Z	U	I	K	T	N	A
F	G	H	E	S	E	E
C	V	V	U	I	D	M
W	A	S	H	L	E	I
S	L	K	O	K	M	T

Rain, Rain and More Rain
Pages 24-25

- The story extract should read:

Noah waited for the triple-decker boat to come to rest on a bit of **land**. There was nothing in sight at first. Nothing but **water** all around. Then at last the mountaintops appeared! Noah sent a **raven** out of the boat. It flew round and round until the water had gone down. Noah sent out a dove, but it found no place to rest and **flew** back to Noah. A week later Noah sent the dove out again. This time it returned with an **olive** branch in its beak. It had found a **tree**!

- There are 7 spiders hiding in the picture.

Abram's Journey Pages 28-29

- Goats A and C are identical.
- Path I leads to the tent.

A Gift from God Pages 32-33

- The odd one out is the fish
- **SARAH** is hidden in the stars.
- The words are

STAR, ABRAM, MORE, CARE, HE, NAMES, MADE and they spell out **ABRAHAM**.

Jacob Plays a Trick Pages 36-37

- **Abraham** and **Isaac** are the two missing names.
- **Isaac** was Jacob's father.

Jacob was Esau's brother.
Rebecca was Isaac's wife.
Esau and **Jacob** were Abraham's grandsons.

- Missing items: **Bow String**, **Arrows**, **Sandal**, **Ear.**
- The answers are circled on the picture.

Joseph's Jealous Brothers Pages 40-41

- Jacob had **twelve** sons.

Jacob had **one** daughter.
Joseph was Jacob's favourite son.
Jacob gave Joseph **a beautiful coat**.
No, Jacob didn't give them presents.
The brothers felt **angry**.
The corn bowed down to Joseph in his first dream.
Yes, Joseph had another dream.
He dreamed about **eleven** stars.
Joseph's brothers wanted to **get rid of him**.

- A **CAMEL** is the animal that is left.

A Slave in Egypt Pages 44-45

- The two brothers are circled on the picture.

- The mistakes are circled on the picture above.
- Joseph number **two** is the correct match.

The Baby in the Basket Pages 48-49

- The words are:

Boys, Moses, Basket, Nile, Bathe, People, Slaves, Miriam, Baby, Palace, Princess, Mother and are circled in the grid.

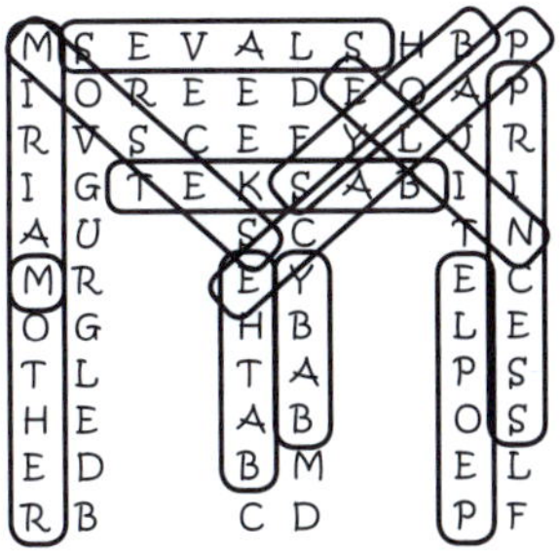

- The beetles are circled on the picture.

Let My People Go Pages 52-53

- The part of the story should read:

One day God said to Moses 'My people are unhappy. I want you to tell the King of Egypt to let them go'

- Blood in the river is **true**.

Mice are **false**.
Insects are **true**.
Snakes are **false**.
Lions are **false**.
Frogs are **true**.
Lizzards are **false**.
Birds are **false**.

- The answers are:

Israelites, Nile, Red, Locusts, The King, Hail, Cows, Houses, Flies, Frogs, and are circled in the grid.

I	J	K	L	I	A	H
S	S	G	O	R	F	V
R	W	A	T	C	H	W
A	O	D	H	F	O	P
E	C	S	E	G	U	H
L	L	E	K	B	S	R
I	R	I	I	C	E	F
T	Y	L	N	D	S	H
E	T	F	G	Y	K	I
S	T	S	U	C	O	L

The Great Escape Pages 56-57

- Fragments: 1D, 2H, 3F, 4I, 5A, 6E.
- The correct spellings are:

'What can we **do** now?' they wailed to Moses. 'If we turn **back**, we will **be** captured by the King. If we go **forwards**, we will surely drown in the Red **Sea**! Moses, why did you bring us here to **die**? Why didn't you **leave** us alone where we were? It is **better** to be a slave than to **die** in the **desert**!'

- The differences are circled on the picture.

Joshua and the Battle of Jericho Page 60-61

- Line **4** is the correct spelling.
- The jumbled lines should read:

I will never leave you.
...thick and impossible to get through.
Guards kept watch day and night.
He listened to God's plan.
The walls of the city collapsed!
We will always serve the Lord.

- The tumbled stones should read:

JOSHUA, MOSES, PRIESTS, GUARDS

- Priest number **3** is the odd one out.

Samuel's Sleepless Night Pages 64-65

Hannah prayed for **a baby**.
God answered Hannah's prayer.
God gave Hannah **a boy**.
The boy was called **Samuel**.
Eli took the boy to live in **God's temple**.
A voice woke the boy up.
The voice said **Samuel**.
The boy ran to **Eli's room**.
The boy ran to Eli's room **three times**.
God wanted to speak with Samuel.
The voice called **Samuel, Samuel**.

- The answers are: **Samuel** and **God**.
- The answers are circled on the picture.

The Shepherd Boy Pages 68-69

• The answers are circled on the picture.

• The answers are circled in the grid.

L	L	L	E	U	M	A	S	H
S	A	I	D	J	I	K	A	B
R	E	M	T	Y	I	N	R	G
D	T	U	B	N	D	J	R	N
R	S	M	G	S	E	N	I	O
E	R	X	O	S	T	V	V	R
H	A	M	S	I	D	P	E	T
P	E	E	R	I	D	E	D	S
E	B	I	V	O	G	E	F	A
H	P	A	G	T	A	H	W	W
S	D	L	E	A	R	S	I	F

• The answer is **ten**.

David and the Giant Pages 72-73

• The answers are circled on the picture.

• The answers are: **Giant, Sword, Soldiers, Scared, Stones, Spear, Sharp, Shouted, David, Sling.**

• The answers are shown in the grid.

		G			W				
	R	O	A	R	E	D		L	
		L			N		D	I	D
	G	I	A	N	T			V	
		A					B	I	G
	S	T	O	N	E	S		N	
F		H				L	E	G	S
O				A		I			H
O		S	T	R	O	N	G		A
D	I	E		M		G			R
		E		Y					P

God Takes Care of Elijah Pages 76-77

• The correct positions are A7, B3, C5, D4, E1, F8, G6, H9, I2

• The answers are: **Drought, Raven, A prophet, Bread, Baal, Firewood, Flour or Oil.**

Fire from Heaven Pages 80-81

• Maths answers are: three **Years,** Hundreds of **Prophets,** One **God.**

• The pairs are: **A-H, B-E, C-F, D-G.**

Naaman and the Little Servant Girl Pages 84-85

• The fragments fit like this: **1-J. 2-F, 3-B, 4-C, 5-A, 6-I.**

• The text should read: 'Go and **wash seven** times in the River **Jordan**. Then you will be healed!'
Naaman was **unhappy**. He thought **Elisha** would at least come out and pray for him.

Daniel in the Lions' Den Pages 88-89

• The answers are circled in the grid.

B	L	O	A	S	N	O	I	L	K
W	A	I	S	H	A	R	P	I	C
O	K	B	V	Y	R	G	N	U	H
R	I	K	Y	E	C	G	W	L	T
S	N	O	T	L	D	R	E	S	E
H	G	H	A	O	O	G	E	U	E
I	V	W	M	N	N	N	B	I	T
P	S	S	G	A	O	N	F	R	H
Y	T	R	I	H	T	S	E	A	V
D	O	G	L	E	I	N	A	D	P

• The word is **Lion**.

Jonah Runs Away Pages 92-93

• The correct answers are:
1) Prophet; 2) Wicked; 3) Ship; 4) Down; 5) Scared; 6) Sea; 7) Fish; 8) Swallowed; 9) Listen: 10) Forgive; 11) High.

• The letters that are left spell: **JONAH.**

• The correct order of the pictues is: **2, 6, 1, 4, 5, 3.**

THE NEW TESTAMENT

MARY'S BABY

God sent the angel Gabriel to a town called Nazareth. He brought news for a young woman named Mary.

'Mary, don't be afraid!' said the angel. 'God has chosen you. You will have a baby boy and you will call Him Jesus. He will be great. He will be the Son of God. His Kingdom will last for ever.'

Mary was amazed. She didn't understand why God had chosen her. But she was happy to obey God.

'I am God's servant,' she said. 'Let it be as you have said.'

Mary was soon going to marry Joseph, a carpenter in Nazareth.

The Roman governor wanted to count all the people in the land. So Joseph had to go to his family's hometown of Bethlehem. Mary went too. It was a long way to travel and Mary's baby was soon to be born. Their donkey carried their bundles of clothes and water bottles.

The road was dry and stony. Mary felt very hot and tired. She hoped they would soon reach their journey's end and have a good rest.

But when they arrived in Bethlehem, there was no room at any inn in the town! Mary was so tired, she was ready to lie down anywhere.

At last, a kind innkeeper offered them shelter in the back of his house, where the animals slept. Mary thanked him and was happy to rest.

That night, Mary's baby was born. She wrapped her little Son in strips of cloth. She laid Him in the soft hay in a manger. She gazed at the baby and remembered what the angel had told her. This was God's own Son. His Kingdom would last for ever.

Jesus had come into the world!

MISSING WORDS

Fill in the missing words, choosing them from the list on the left. Be careful – there are five words that do not belong in the passage!

PRINCE
SON
STABLE
MARY
ANGEL
JOSEPH
CARPENTER
GOD
GABRIEL
TOWN
QUEEN
DONKEY
BABY
NAZARETH
DAVID
PLANNING

Mary lived in the little __________ of __________. She was __________ to marry a __________ named JOSEPH. One day the __________ __________ came to ______. '______ is pleased with you,' said Gabriel. 'You are going to have a ______. He will be called the ______ of God. He will be a great King like ________.'

Crossword

Fill in the answers using the picture clues.

3 ACROSS

5 ACROSS

6 ACROSS

8 ACROSS

1 DOWN

2 DOWN

4 DOWN

7 DOWN

THE ANGELS AND THE SHEPHERDS

On the hills near Bethlehem, shepherds were looking after their sheep. It was a clear night and the shepherds looked up at the stars.

Suddenly, the sky was filled with a blinding light. An angel of the Lord appeared!

'Don't be afraid!' said the angel. 'I bring good news and great joy to you! Tonight in Bethlehem your Saviour has been born! He is Christ the Lord. This is how you will know it is Him – you will find the baby lying in a manger, wrapped in strips of cloth.'

The sky was filled with angels, singing praises to God:

'Glory to God in the highest heaven, and on earth peace and goodwill to all!'

It was a glorious sight!

The shepherds knew what they must do. They left their sheep at once and

hurried down into the town.

'We must see this thing that God has told us about!' they said.

They found Mary and Joseph and the baby lying in the manger. This was their Saviour!

'It is all just as the angel said!' they exclaimed.

Mary heard how the angels had appeared to the shepherds and she treasured their words in her heart.

The shepherds went back to their sheep, singing songs of praise to God and telling everyone about the wonderful things they had seen.

SPOT THE DIFFERENCE

Put a circle around each of the ten differences between the two pictures.

FIND THE HIDDEN WORD

Unscramble each of the following words and put them in the boxes alongside. When complete, the shaded boxes will reveal something from the story. The first one has been done to help you.

SAW	W	A	S					
EACH								
GLEAN								
CAPE FUEL								
THAW								
GERMAN								
RIFE								
TRIED								
DAIS						Answer:		

COMPLETE THE PICTURE

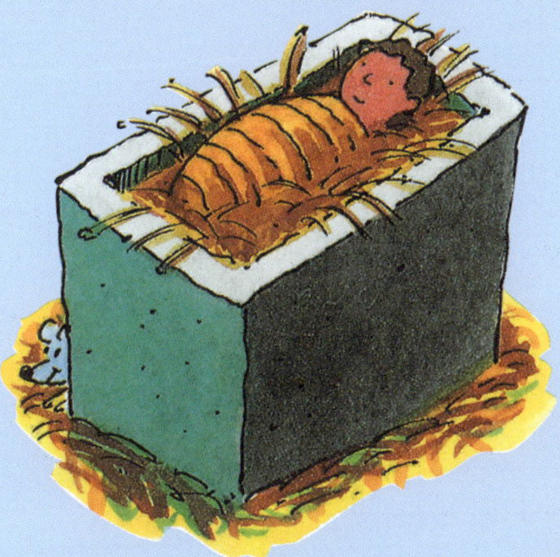

Copy the small picture to complete the big picture.

THE JOURNEY OF THE WISE MEN

Wise men in an eastern country were studying the stars.

They had spotted a new star, shining brightly in the sky.

'It means a new King has been born!' they said. 'We must travel west and find Him. We will take gifts to honour Him!'

The wise men set off across the desert, following the star.

The star seemed to have stopped over the city of Jerusalem. The wise men found the palace of King Herod and asked to see the new baby King.

But Herod knew nothing about a new King. The teachers of the Law looked in their scrolls. 'It is written here that a leader will come from Bethlehem!'

So the wise men set off again to Bethlehem. King Herod wanted them to return and tell him when they had found the new King. But he didn't want to honour Him. He wanted to get rid of Him!

The wise men reached Bethlehem.

'Look! The star is shining over there!' they said, pointing to a poor house.

They went quietly into the house and found Mary with her little Son Jesus.

The wise men knelt down before the boy and worshipped Him.

'We have found the new King!' they said.

They took out their gifts to give to Jesus: gold, frankincense and myrrh.

Mary looked at the gifts in wonder and amazement.

When it was time to leave, God warned them in a dream to go home by another road. Mary and Joseph took Jesus away from Bethlehem to safety in Egypt. The boy grew up there until King Herod had died and it was safe to return.

King Herod did not find Him there.

PICTURE SETS

Can you match up the four sets of pictures? Put a ring round them as you find them. All are hidden in the grid, either horizontally or vertically.

1

2

3

4

Hidden Words

Hidden in the letters below are twelve words that can also be found in the story. Cross out each one as you find it and then circle them in the grid. The remaining letters in the grid will spell out something about the story.

PRHUBETHLEHEMVXBOYAOAJHUIFKHERODLOPNBHFJESUS
BVYTUEKSJERUSALEMBVHFYITASLMYRRHOPLFDWISEMEN
STARLODJFGOLDKORFMARYICKPKENSEPALACEXMEKINGW

B	M	Y	R	R	H	T	H	R
E	E	E	J	O	U	R	A	N
T	C	D	L	O	G	T	E	Y
H	A	O	F	N	S	H	T	H
L	L	W	I	S	E	M	E	N
E	A	K	Y	R	U	E	W	I
H	P	O	O	S	E	S	M	E
E	B	D	M	A	R	Y	E	N
M	E	L	A	S	U	R	E	J

ANSWER:

THE FOUR FISHERMEN

Jesus grew up and began to talk to people about God.

One day, He was standing on the shore of Lake Gennesaret. He saw two fishing boats near the shore. The fishermen had pulled the boats on to the sandy beach and were washing their nets.

Jesus asked if He could stand in one of the boats and talk to the crowd of people who had come to listen to Him. People were pushing and jostling each other. They all wanted to listen to Jesus.

The boat Jesus picked out belonged to Simon and Andrew. They were happy to let Jesus stand in their boat.

When Jesus had finished speaking, He told Simon to push the boat out and let down the fishing nets.

'Master,' said Simon, 'we have fished all night but caught nothing. Not even a squid. But if You say so, we'll try again.'

Simon let down the nets one more time. Suddenly the nets were filled with an enormous catch of fish! They slapped and slithered about in the net so hard that it nearly broke! Simon called to his friends, James and John, in the other boat to come and help.

Simon was amazed and fell at Jesus' feet.

'Don't be afraid,' said Jesus. 'Follow Me!'

So Simon, Andrew, James and John left their nets and followed Jesus. They were His first disciples.

WHAT'S HIDDEN IN THE NETS?

Find the nine letters hidden in the fishing net.

Unscramble the letters to spell out something from the story.

CHECK OUT THE DETAIL

Identify and tick the five details below that come from this picture.

1	2	3	4	5	6	7	8	9

JESUS MEETS MATTHEW

Everyone hated tax collectors. They often took more money than they needed and kept the extra money for themselves. They made themselves richer while ordinary people became poorer.

Matthew was collecting taxes when he first met Jesus.

'Come, follow Me!' invited Jesus.

Matthew did not need to be asked twice. Without looking back, he left his booth and joined the growing number of men whom Jesus had called to be His friends and disciples.

Many of these men were fishermen. Matthew did not really fit in. But he knew that he belonged where Jesus was.

Then Matthew held a great feast in his house and invited Jesus. There was wonderful food and wine. It was a huge celebration. Matthew invited many different guests, including tax collectors.

Teachers of the Law grumbled about this, asking, 'Why do Jesus and His friends eat and drink with the tax collectors? No one likes them!'

Jesus heard what they were saying and answered, 'Healthy people do not need a doctor. These people need My help.'

Matthew became a special disciple of Jesus and followed Him wherever He went. His whole life was going to change for ever.

Matthew had spent his life counting money and taxes. Now he would follow Jesus and leave his money behind.

CRACK THE CODE

Using the following code, can you work out the questions? Then write the answers in the boxes.

1	2	3	4	5	6	7	8	9	10	11	12	13
Z	Y	X	W	V	U	T	S	R	Q	P	O	N
14	15	16	17	18	19	20	21	22	23	24	25	26
M	L	K	J	I	H	G	F	E	D	C	B	A

4 19 26 7 4 26 8 14 26 7 7 19 22 4 ?

The decoded question:

The answer:

4 19 22 9 22 23 18 23 17 22 8 6 8 22 26 7 ?

The decoded question:

The answer:

4 19 12 20 9 6 14 25 15 22 23 ?

The decoded question:

The answer:

4 19 26 7 23 18 23 14 26 7 7 19 22 4 25 22 24 12 14 22 ?

The decoded question:

The answer:

TWO OF A KIND

Circle the five things
that appear in both of these pictures.

THE FOUR KIND FRIENDS

Jesus was inside a house, talking to teachers of the Law. The room was very crowded and no one else could squeeze inside.

Suddenly four men arrived at the house, carrying another on a mat between them. The man on the mat could not walk. He couldn't even sit up. He desperately needed help – and the four friends believed that Jesus could give it.

But the friends could not get through the crowd to Jesus.

'Let's try the roof!' said one of them.

They had made their way to where Jesus was. They were sure that if they could get to Jesus, Jesus would heal him.

So the men began to scrape away at the mud between the branches that made up the flat roof. Bits of dirt and twigs fell down on the people in the room below.

Soon everyone stopped talking in the room and watched as the hole grew from a tiny one to a large gap big enough to lower the man and his mat down in front of Jesus!

Jesus could see they had faith in Him. He turned to the man on the mat.

'My son, your sins are forgiven.'

'What is He saying?" muttered the teachers of the Law. 'How can He forgive sins? Only God can do that!'

Jesus knew what they were saying and turned to them. 'I will show you that the Son of Man can forgive sins.'

Jesus turned to the man on the mat and said, 'Pick up your mat and walk! Go home now.'

Everyone watched in amazement as the man got up off the floor, rolled up his mat and walked out of the house!

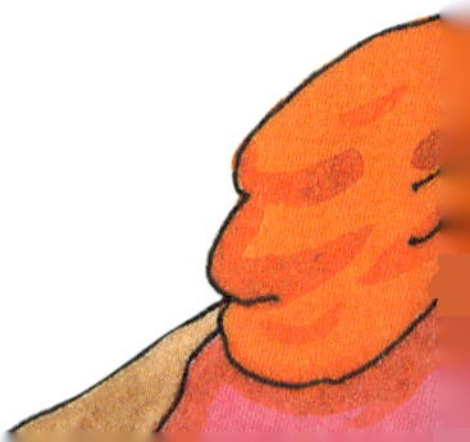

TRUE OR FALSE?

If true put a tick in the box, if false put a cross.

The man did not have any friends.	A
The man had been sick for only one day.	B
The men made a hole in the roof.	C
Jesus climbed through the roof.	D
The man had a bad arm.	E
The house was full of people.	F
The rope broke.	G
Jesus made the man well.	H

CAN YOU COMPLETE AND FIX THE PICTURE?

THE STORY OF THE TWO HOUSES

Jesus told many stories to the crowds who followed Him. Sometimes you could almost imagine the story in pictures.

One day He told this story:

'If you listen to My words and obey them, you will be like a wise man who built his house upon a rock.

'It took a long time for the man to build his house. He had to dig down deep to make strong foundations. He used strong stone to build the walls of the house. He sweated and worked very hard. At last it was finished. The man moved in and felt safe.

'In the winter, the weather turned bad!

The rain poured down, strong winds blew, the rivers flooded and many houses were washed away. But the house on the rock stood firm. Its foundations were strong and deep. The man was happy and knew that it was worth all that hard work.

'But if you don't listen to My words, you are like a foolish man. He built his house on the shifting sand.

'"I don't think I can be bothered to make this house very strong!" said the man. "I want to move in quickly. I don't think it will matter too much if the foundations are a bit near the surface. I just want to get the house ready before the winter."

'He was a lazy man. But his house was soon ready and the man moved in.

'But when winter came, so did the bad weather! The rain came down, the wind blew hard, the rivers flooded. The foolish man noticed cracks in his walls. The cracks grew bigger and bigger and bigger, then CRASH! The house came tumbling down and was washed away by the rains!'

FIND THE WORDS

Fill in the missing words using those from the list below.
Be careful: some of the words don't belong!

WISE
STORY
BUS
SHELTER
FIELD
RIVER
CINEMA
BUILD
HOUSE
SEA
MAN
PLEASED
STONE
ROCK
HARD
LONG
FINISHED

Once Jesus told a ________ about a ________

man who wanted to ________ a ________ .

'Where shall I build it?' the ________ wondered.

'Shall I build it near the ________ ?

Shall I build it near the ________ ?

Shall I build it in a ________ ?

No! I will build it on solid ________ .'

The wise man began to build. He worked ________ .

He worked for a ________ time.

When his house was ________ he was ________ .

COMPLETE THE STORY

Can you put all the vowels, **a, e, i, o** and **u**, back into this section from the story so that it makes sense again?

'_f y__ l_st_n t_ my w_rds _nd _b_y th_m, y__ w_ll b_ l_k_ _ w_s_ m_n wh_ b__lt h_s h__s_ _p_n _ r_ck.'

Whose house would you rather live in?
The hard working man's or the lazy man's.

Answer: ....

THE BIG STORM

One day, Jesus got into a boat with His friends. It had been a tiring day.

'Let's go over to the other side of Lake Galilee,' said Jesus.

Many of Jesus' disciples were fishermen. They knew about boats. Very soon, the water against the side of the boat sent Jesus to sleep.

After they had been sailing for a little while, the wind changed and some black clouds moved quickly across the sky. Soon a mighty storm was blowing. The boat was rocked about and began to fill with water!

Jesus was still fast asleep. His head was on a pillow. He didn't seem to notice the storm and the rocking boat at all!

'Wake up! Wake up!' the disciples called to Jesus. They had started to panic. 'We are all going to drown!'

Jesus woke up. He stood up on the deck. He spoke to the winds and commanded them to stop blowing. He spoke to the waves and ordered them to be calm.

All at once the storm vanished. The lake was completely calm again.

Then Jesus turned to His disciples and said, 'Why were you so afraid? Don't you trust Me?'

The disciples were amazed. They looked at one another and said, 'Who can this Man be? Even the winds and waves obey Him!'

WORD PUZZLE

The lists of words below are all to do with the story but have letters missing. Choosing from the collection of letters, put them into their correct spaces and then find the words on the grid. They may be forwards, backwards, up, down or diagonally.

DISCI_L_S	HI_HER	LO_E_	JE___S	S_A
LA_E	RO_K_D	PI_ _OW	WE_T	SH_O_
A_AK_	DRO_N	W_VES	STO_M	W_N_
CA_M	E_CIT_D	FA_T	RES_	BO_T
H_LP	C_O_S	HO_LI_G	S_NK	ST_OD
A_RA_D	I_PO_TANT			

P	E	R	R
G	L	I	S
E	L	D	W
W	N	L	N
R	O	X	I
U	K	E	O
S	W	S	F
E	E	T	I
K	W	A	M
C	A	E	R

H	L	S	E	L	P	I	C	S	I	D	B
K	O	R	Y	X	R	E	H	G	I	H	O
S	W	W	E	V	C	D	I	A	R	F	A
E	E	R	L	S	P	I	L	L	O	W	T
V	R	A	O	I	T	S	T	Z	O	W	N
A	P	W	K	C	N	J	S	E	E	I	A
W	F	A	W	O	K	G	E	O	D	N	T
L	A	K	E	S	P	E	M	S	R	D	R
A	S	E	N	H	J	H	D	L	U	C	O
E	T	S	T	O	O	D	S	W	A	S	P
S	I	N	K	O	N	W	O	R	D	C	M
P	L	E	H	K	S	T	O	R	M	M	I

How many?

Look back at the picture on page 129.

How many people are in the boat?

How many oars can you see?

How many people are wearing stripes?

How many people have their heads covered?

How many people are pulling on the oar?

Now add all the numbers to get a TOTAL

A

C

B

D

Which of these people sailed in the boat?

Tick the boxes to show who was in the boat.

E

F

G

THE GIRL WHO CAME BACK TO LIFE

Crowds of people followed Jesus wherever He went. A man called Jairus called out from the crowd:

'Jesus! Please help me! My only daughter is dying! We need your help!'

As Jesus made His way to Jairus' house, He stopped to heal a woman who had been ill for many years. The crowds were pressing all around Jesus and He couldn't get through very quickly.

Just then, a messenger came from Jairus' household to say, 'It's too late. The girl has already died.'

But Jesus said to Jairus, 'Don't be

afraid. Believe in Me and she will be well.'

When He arrived at Jairus' house, everyone was crying and wailing loudly. It was a terrible sight.

'Don't worry,' said Jesus kindly, 'she is not dead. She is just sleeping.'

He went into the house with Peter, John and James and spoke to the girl.

'Get up, My child,' He said gently. At once, life returned to her body and she sat up! It was a miracle.

Jesus told her parents to give the girl something to eat and look after her.

They couldn't believe their eyes, but were overjoyed to see their twelve-year-old daughter alive again.

They thanked Jesus with all their hearts.

Can you spell?

Each of the following words has only one correct spelling and all the others are incorrect. Tick which one you think is correct.

☐ JARIUS	☐ JAIRUS	☐ JIRUS	☐ JIROUS
☐ DOKTORS	☐ DOCTORS	☐ DOKTERS	☐ DOCKTORS
☐ PLEASE	☐ PLEESE	☐ PLEAS	☐ PLEES
☐ DAUHTER	☐ DAUTER	☐ DAWTER	☐ DAUGHTER
☐ BELIEVE	☐ BELEAVE	☐ BELIVE	☐ BELEIVE
☐ MESSENGER	☐ MESSANGER		
☐ COULD	☐ COOD		
☐ ROOME	☐ ROOM		
☐ MIRACLE	☐ MIRRACLE		
☐ TWELEVE	☐ TWELVE		

CRACK THE CODE

Using the following code, can you work out the questions? Then write the answers in the boxes.

1	2	3	4	5	6	7	8	9	10	11	12	13
Z	Y	X	W	V	U	T	S	R	Q	P	O	N
14	15	16	17	18	19	20	21	22	23	24	25	26
M	L	K	J	I	H	G	F	E	D	C	B	A

4 19 12 4 26 8 23 2 18 13 20 ?

The decoded question:

The answer:

4 19 12 23 18 23 17 22 8 6 8 19 22 26 15 ?

The decoded question:

The answer:

4 19 12 4 22 13 7 4 18 7 19 17 22 8 6 8 ?

The decoded question:

The answer:

19 12 4 12 15 23 4 26 8 7 19 22 20 18 9 15 ?

The decoded question:

The answer:

THE LIVING BREAD

Jesus and His disciples had been busy all day. People everywhere wanted to see Jesus. They had heard how He could make sick people well again so they brought with them their old and unwell relatives. They wanted to hear what He said about God's Kingdom. They wanted to know how much God loved them.

Now the sun was beginning to set and there were still great crowds of people all around. They were in no hurry to go home.

'We must send the people off to get food in the villages,' said the disciples. 'They are hungry.'

But Jesus replied, 'They can eat here. We must give them some food.'

'But there are thousands of people here!' said one of them. 'No one could possibly afford to feed them all!'

'There is a young boy here with his packed lunch,' said another. 'But all he has is five loaves and two fish,' said Andrew. 'That will never be enough to feed all these people.'

Jesus smiled and took the loaves and fishes. He told the disciples to make the people sit in groups of about fifty people.

Then Jesus gave thanks to God for the food and broke it into pieces. He gave them to the disciples to share out among the crowd.

Everyone passed the food to another and shared it between them. Everyone ate and had more than enough. It was a great feast.

At the end, the disciples gathered up enough leftovers to fill twelve baskets.

'I am the bread of life,' said Jesus later. 'Whoever comes to Me will never be hungry; whoever believes in Me will never be thirsty.'

Picture Puzzle

There are five differences between these two pictures. Put a circle around each of them.

I SPY

The fish seem to get into the strangest places. How many can you see?

- [ ] 1) I spy a fish in a bird's mouth.
- [ ] 2) I spy a striped fish.
- [ ] 3) I spy a child holding up a fish.
- [ ] 4) I spy a goat with a fish in its mouth.
- [ ] 5) I spy a man with a fish in his head-dress band.
- [ ] 6) I spy a child holding a fish.
- [ ] 7) I spy two men holding up a fish.
- [ ] 8) I spy a woman eating a fish.
- [ ] 9) I spy a fish peeping from a woman's robe.
- [ ] 10) I spy a fish on a man's hat.
- [ ] 11) I spy a fish on a woman's knee.
- [ ] 12) I spy a fish on a mountainside.

THE GOOD NEIGHBOUR

'Love God with all your heart,' said Jesus. 'Love your neighbour as much as you love yourself!' said Jesus.

'But who is my neighbour?' asked a man.

To answer the question, Jesus told the man this story.

'A man was once travelling down the road from Jerusalem to Jericho when he was attacked by robbers. They took his money and his clothes and hurt him so badly that he couldn't move. He lay beside the road in the heat of the day for hours and hours. He was sure he would die if no one came to help him.

'Then a man came towards him.

'"At last!" thought the injured man. "Help has come!"

But the man walked on past him as if he hadn't even noticed him.

'Another man approached. "Surely this man will help me!" thought the man, his head throbbing with pain. But the second man walked past him too. He pretended he couldn't see him at all.

'"Now I must surely die!" wailed the man. The sun was beating down on his wounded head.

'Just then a third man, a Samaritan, came down the road. As soon as he saw the wounded man, he rushed up to him.

'"What happened to you?" he asked. "Let me help you."

'The Samaritan gave him something to drink, bandaged his wounds, and lifted

him on to his own donkey. He took the man to an inn where the Samaritan paid the innkeeper two silver coins to look after him.

'"Look after him," he told the innkeeper. "If he costs you any more than this, I will pay you when I return."

'Now,' said Jesus. 'Who was the poor man's neighbour?'

'The one who was kind to him,' replied the man.

'Yes. Go and do the same,' said Jesus.

SPOT THE DIFFERENCE

Can you spot ten differences between these two pictures?

CAN YOU COPY THE PICTURE?

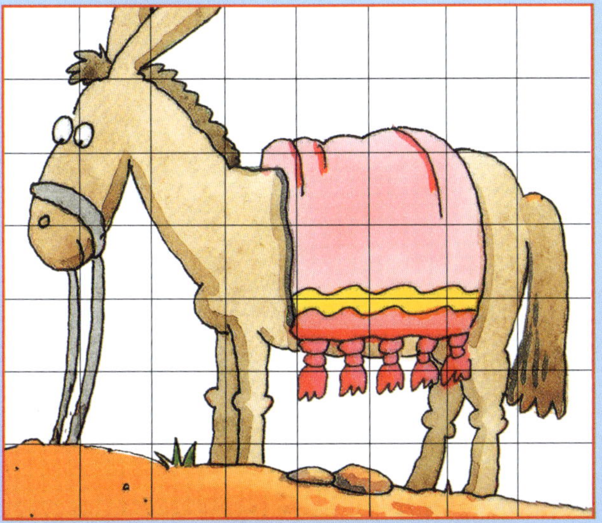

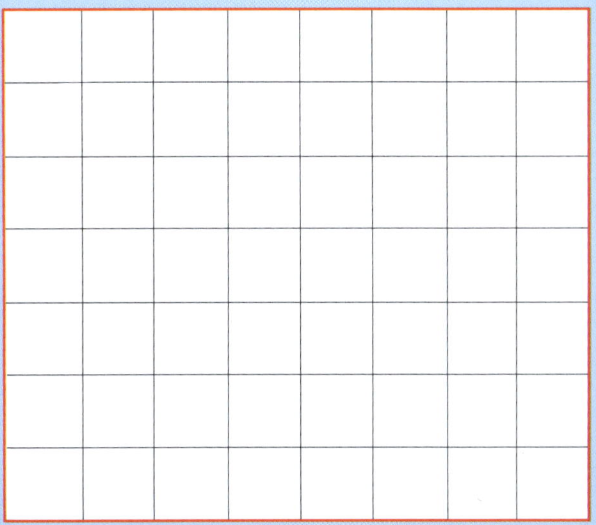

CAN YOU FIND TWELVE MISTAKES IN THIS EXTRACT FROM THE STORY?

'Just then a fourth man, a Samaritanian, came down the motorway. As soon as he saw the wounded man, he rushed up to him. "What happened to you?" he asked. "Let me call an ambulance."

'The Samaritanian gave him something to read, bandaged his donkey, and lifted him into a tree. He took the man to a hospital where the Samaritanian paid an cleaner two camels to look after him.

THE STORY OF THE LOST SHEEP

Jesus once told this story about a shepherd:

'A shepherd once had a hundred sheep. He knew them all and looked after them very well. If wild animals came close, the shepherd chased them away. He did everything he could to protect his sheep.

'One day, the shepherd counted his sheep and found that one was missing! Where could it be?

'He set out from the sheepfold to look for the lost sheep. He left the other ninety-nine safely penned in the fold.

'The shepherd looked everywhere: behind bushes, near the stream, behind rocks and in craggy places. No sign of the missing sheep.

'Suddenly there came a faint bleating sound. Was it the lost sheep?

'Yes! The shepherd had found his lost sheep at last.

'Gently, the shepherd put the lost sheep on his shoulders and carried it carefully home to the sheepfold.

'He was so pleased to find his lost sheep that he held a party and invited all his neighbours. They knew how much he loved his sheep.

'God is a bit like that shepherd,' said Jesus. 'He cares if any one of His sheep is lost. The angels in heaven rejoice and sing when anyone on earth says sorry to God for the wrong things they have done.'

Counting sheep

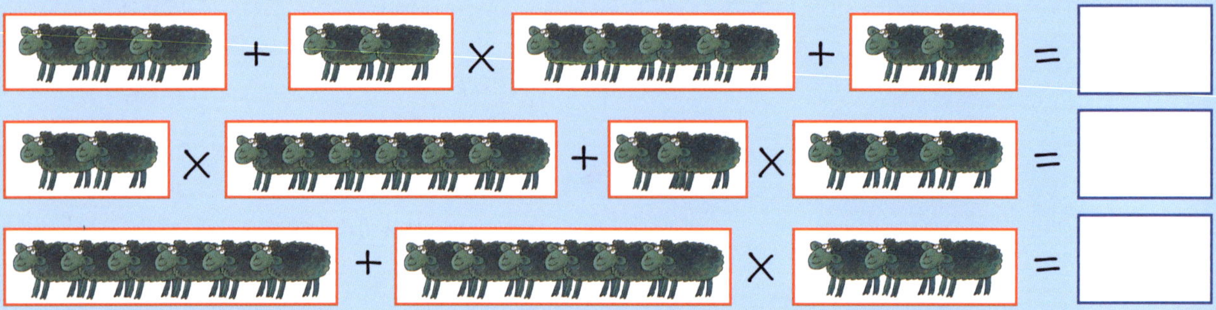

How many sheep did the shepherd have?

If the shepherd lost one sheep how many would he have left?

If half the sheep went missing how many would be left?

If ten sheep went missing how many would be left if the shepherd then found five?

If twenty sheep went missing how many would be left if the shepherd then found fifteen?

If seventy sheep hid in the woods and five hid in the bushes how many would be left?

If forty sheep ran away and five more got lost how many would be left?

Maze Muddle

Find the path that leads to the lost sheep.

THE MAN WHO COULD NOT SEE

A poor blind man had been sitting at the roadside every day of his life. He listened for the sound of a coin or two clinking in his begging bowl. But today none came. Where was everybody? He could hear crowds of people going past but nobody stopped.

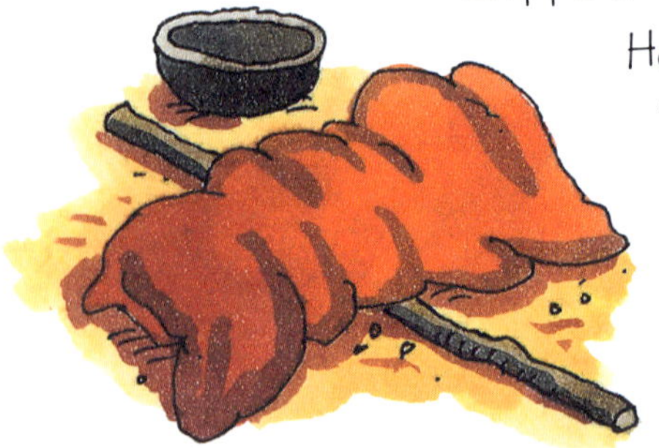

He heard a name. 'Jesus!' 'Let's see Jesus!' 'Jesus can heal people!'

The man, who was called Bartimaeus, got to his feet.

'Jesus! Take pity on me!' he shouted as loudly as he possibly could.

'Be quiet, blind man!' grumbled people in the crowd.

'Bring the blind man to Me,' Jesus said firmly. 'What do you want Me to do for you?' asked Jesus kindly.

'I want to see!' he sighed.

'Then see!' said Jesus. 'You believe I can

help you. Your faith has made you well!'

All at once, the man's eyes became bright and clear and the world was full of colour and movement.

'Thanks be to God!' shouted the man. 'I can see! I can see!'

The crowd saw what had happened and joined him in praising God for the wonderful thing Jesus had done.

TRUE OR FALSE?

For the first time Bartimaeus could see the crowd around him. Tick the boxes to show which of these people he saw.

JUMBLED WORDS

The boxes below contain jumbled letters and a question mark. Use the spare letters in the white box to complete each word, and then rearrange the letters to reveal the secret message.

U R E I H N R M S S T

H N W ?	?	E E D ?	E L P ?

O L D ?	J E S U ?	M D N I ? E	E ?

O ?	A K ?	O Y ?

What did Bartimaeus ask of Jesus?

____

____

THE LITTLE TAX COLLECTOR

Zacchaeus was a tax collector. No one liked him. In fact he had cheated many people and stolen money. He was not a popular man at all.

But one day, Jesus was passing through Jericho and Zacchaeus wanted to see Him. He had heard great things about Jesus and wanted to see Him with his own eyes.

Crowds of people lined the streets. Zacchaeus was very short, however, and could not hope to see Jesus unless he was above the crowd. He spotted a sycomore tree.

'I'll climb that tree!' said Zacchaeus to himself. 'If I can sit above the crowd, I ought to be able to see Jesus when He comes past.'

He didn't have to wait long. Jesus was on His way!

As Jesus came close, Zacchaeus leaned out of the branches to get a good look. Jesus was coming! Then suddenly Zacchaeus nearly fell out of the tree in amazement! Jesus had stopped beneath the tree and was calling up to him in the branches!

'Zacchaeus, hurry down!' said Jesus, 'I must stay and eat at your house today.'

Zacchaeus climbed down and greeted Jesus with great joy. He could hardly believe it. Why would Jesus want to speak to him? Nobody else ever did!

'You are most welcome to my house,' said Zacchaeus.

Zacchaeus was a changed man. He later told Jesus, 'I will give half of all I own to the poor. If I have cheated anyone, I will pay him back four times as much.'

He kept his word.

'The Son of Man came to find and to save the lost,' said Jesus. 'This man has come back to God's kingdom.'

COMPLETE THE WORDS

The following words are incomplete. Some have their beginnings, middles or ends missing. Can you use the words in the box below to complete them? The first one has been done to show you. When you have the complete words, find them in the grid on the next page. Words can be placed forwards, backwards, up, down or diagonally.

SH**OR**T	RE _ _ _ _ D	FOL _ _ _ ING
HO _ _ _	SYCOM _ _ _	M _ _ _ Y
JES _ _	D _ _ _ ER	_ _ OD
T _ _ _ K	PU _ _ _ D	G _ _ _ _ Y
JE _ _ _ _ O	CH _ _ _	

ACHE	EAT	ONE	USE	~~OR~~	GO	SHE	ORE
INN	REED	RICH	RUN	LOW	US		

Wordsearch

D	D	I	D	S	Y	C	O	M	O	R	E	B
O	Y	O	A	M	P	O	H	C	I	R	E	J
M	O	N	E	Y	C	U	U	G	C	A	S	C
G	R	E	E	D	Y	H	S	A	D	C	U	T
O	H	O	U	S	E	E	E	H	H	H	S	R
S	R	D	I	N	N	E	R	A	E	T	E	O
F	O	L	L	O	W	I	N	G	T	D	J	H
R	E	A	C	H	E	D	T	R	U	N	K	S

THE KING ON A DONKEY

It was time for the Passover festival when people remembered the time when God had rescued Moses and the Israelites from slavery in Egypt.

Jesus spent a few days with His friends Martha, Mary and Lazarus in Bethany. Then He set off for the city of Jerusalem.

Jesus sent two friends ahead of Him. 'Go to the village over there. You will find a young donkey that has never been ridden before. Bring it to Me. If the owner asks

what you are doing, tell him that your master needs it.'

They went to the village and saw the young donkey. They were just untying it when the owner said, 'What are you doing with my donkey?'

'The Master needs it!' they said.

They took the donkey to Jesus and put their cloaks on the donkey's back. Then Jesus rode into Jerusalem.

Great crowds of people cheered for Jesus and waved palm branches and spread their cloaks on the road.

'Hosanna!' they cried in a loud voice. 'God bless the king who comes in the name of the Lord!'

PICTURE PUZZLE

There are ten differences between these two pictures. Can you find them all?

WORD PUZZLE

Jesus promised the people two things before He died. To find out what they are, use the code below.

A	B	C	D	E	F	G
3	6	9	12	15	18	21
H	I	J	K	L	M	N
24	27	30	33	36	39	42
O	P	Q	R	S	T	U
45	48	51	54	57	60	63
V	W	X	Y	Z		
66	69	72	75	78		

60 24 27 57   27 57   39 75   6 45 12 75   69 24 27 9 24   27

69 27 36 36   21 27 66 15   63 48   18 45 54   75 45 63

60 24 27 57   27 57   39 75   6 36 45 45 12   69 24 27 9 24   27

69 27 36 36   57 24 15 12   18 45 54   75 45 63

Picture Maze

Can you help the donkey lead Jesus into Jerusalem?

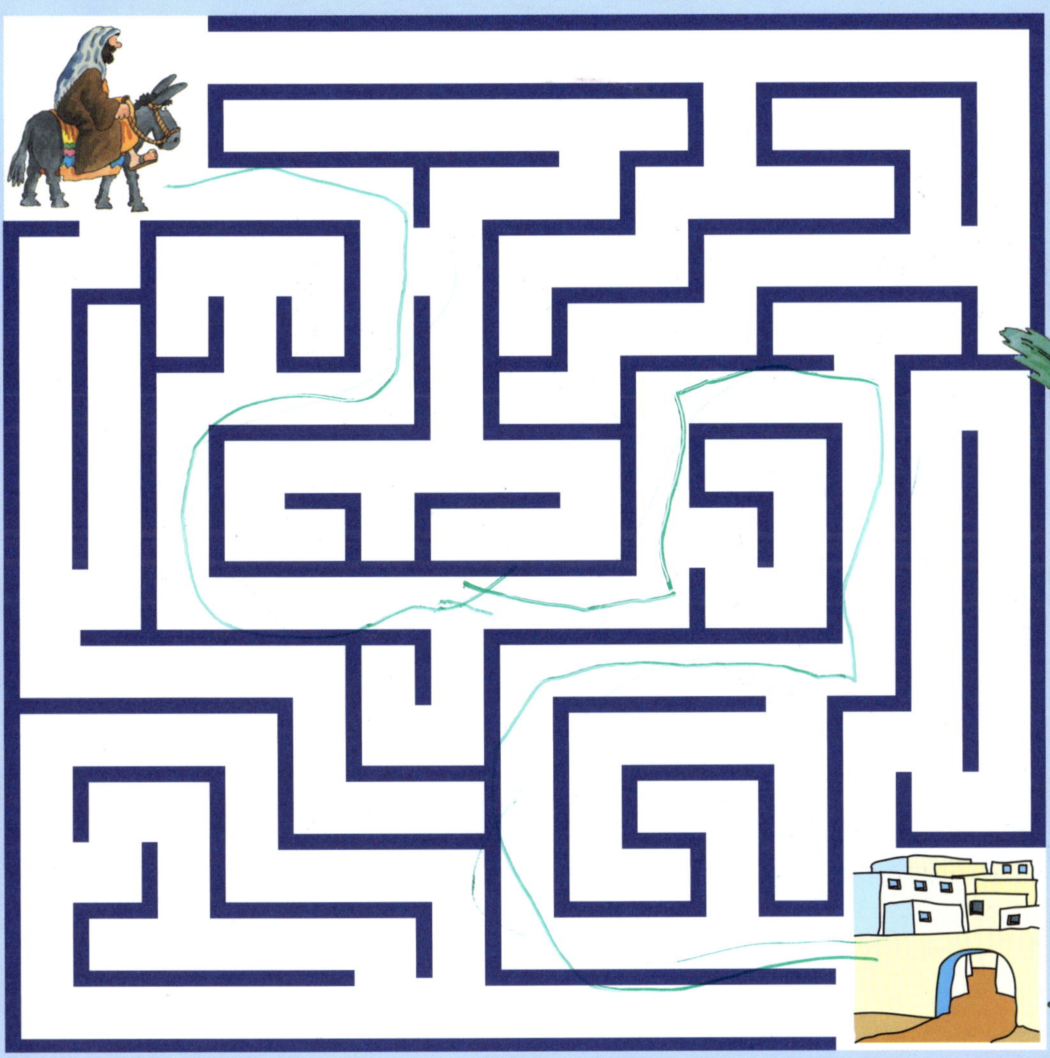

JESUS IS CRUCIFIED

Jesus had many friends but He also had enemies. They wanted to get rid of Him.

Jesus knew that He was going to die, but He shared one last special meal with His disciples and washed their feet.

Jesus took a cup of wine, gave thanks

to God and passed it round to His friends. 'Take this and drink,' He said to them.

Then Jesus took a piece of bread, broke it and gave it to the others, saying, 'This is My body, given for you. Do this and remember Me.'

They didn't understand what Jesus meant. They didn't understand when He told them He would soon be going away from them.

Jesus had done nothing wrong, but He was arrested. The soldiers were cruel to Him, beat Him and made Him wear a purple robe. They put a crown of thorns on His head.

'People call You a king!' they mocked.

Jesus had to carry a heavy cross to a hill called Golgotha. Two criminals were going to be put on crosses next to Jesus. But Jesus had done nothing wrong.

Above His head was a sign saying: King of the Jews.

Jesus' mother, Mary, and His best friends stood close by and watched. They hated to see Him suffering.

Jesus was put on a cross and left to die.

Darkness covered the land. At the ninth hour, Jesus cried out to God in a loud voice, then He died.

Jesus' body was taken down from the cross and put in a tomb in the rock. A large stone was rolled across the door of the tomb.

It was a terrible day.

Picture Puzzle

There are twelve small wooden crosses hidden in this picture. Can you draw a circle around them?

WORD PUZZLE

Written below is a selection of words to do with the story. Each one has its own definition or meaning. Can you match them up and write the correct word below.

WRONG ANGRY ARRESTED WISHED PAID NAILED STUMBLED NEAR HEAVY ENTRANCE HIT THOUGHT

DEFINITION	WORD
1) Captured and held briefly	ARRESTED
2) When something is not right	
3) Feeling cross	
4) Longed for something in particular	
5) Settled a debt	
6) Walked unsteadily	
7) When something is hard to carry	
8) At a short distance away	
9) A place of entry	
10) To deal a blow or strike someone	
11) Considered something	
12) Fastened something with a nail	

JESUS IS ALIVE

Three days had passed since Jesus had died on the cross.

Jesus' disciples were terribly sad. Their friend and master had left them.

Other people were sad too, including a group of women.

On the third day, the women went to visit the tomb. They took herbs and spices to put on Jesus' body. That was the custom in those days when someone had died.

But when they reached the tomb, they had a big shock! They found that the heavy stone had been rolled away from the entrance.

The women were afraid. They looked into the tomb. The body was gone! Where was Jesus? Who had taken Him?

Suddenly, two men in bright shining clothes appeared at the entrance.

The women bowed down to the ground, full of fear and trembling. Then the men spoke to the women, saying, 'Why are you looking for Jesus here? He is not dead, He is alive! Remember what He told you before He left you?'

The women tried to remember. Jesus had said many things they didn't understand. He had said He was leaving

them, but yes, He had said He would come back! Could it really be true?

The women ran to tell the disciples as fast as they could.

'Jesus is alive!' they said. 'The tomb is empty!'

The disciples did not believe the women. Peter ran to the tomb to see for himself. He saw the cloths that Jesus' body had been wrapped in, but sure enough, Jesus was not there!

Not long afterwards, Jesus appeared to His disciples and they knew that Jesus really was alive again!

Picture puzzle

There are ten differences between these pictures. Draw a circle around each of them.

Word puzzle

Find the words below in the grid. The remaining letters will spell out an important person in the story.

FRIDAY	ANGELS	SATURDAY
AFTERNOON	JESUS	CRY
FRIENDS	RAN	STONE
ENTRANCE	MAN	PLEASE
TOMB	OPEN	GOOD
TWO	ROLLED	GARDENER
EYES	NEWS	

E	S	A	T	U	R	D	A	Y	M
C	A	R	Y	G	O	B	M	O	T
N	F	S	M	A	A	A	C	R	Y
A	F	T	E	R	N	O	O	N	A
R	G	O	O	D	N	G	E	Y	D
T	E	N	D	E	A	S	A	E	R
N	Y	E	P	N	A	D	L	O	U
E	E	O	G	E	I	L	W	S	T
A	S	E	L	R	O	T	W	L	A
A	L	P	F	R	I	E	N	D	S
S	U	S	E	J	N	B	M	O	T

The important person is: ____________

Which two words are entered in the grid twice? __________ __________

Word puzzle

Here are lots of words to do with the story and their opposite meanings. Match them up by drawing a line between them. Be careful, there are a few words that shouldn't be there!

BACK	SITTING
SIDE	CRIED
HAPPY	EXIT
LAUGHED	EMPTY
ALIVE	LIGHT
ENEMIES	SAD
OUTSIDE	INSIDE
WASN'T	CLEAN
ENTRANCE	FRONT
DARK	NOTHING
FULL	DEAD
DOWN	WAS
STANDING	BAD
SOMETHING	FRIENDS

THOMAS BELIEVES

It was late on the Sunday evening that Jesus appeared to His disciples. They were meeting in a room in the town and had locked the doors tightly. They were afraid that they might be arrested because they had followed Jesus.

Suddenly Jesus was there in the room with them.

'Peace be with you,' He said. He showed them the wounds in His hands and His side. There was no doubt about it. This was Jesus!

Thomas was not there that day. When his friends told him the good news, he could not believe it.

'But we have seen Him!' said his friends.

'Well, unless I can *see* His hands and feet and the marks where He was nailed to the cross, I won't *believe* it,' answered Thomas.

A week later, Thomas and all the disciples were gathered together and had locked all the doors.

Suddenly, Jesus was there in the room with them! 'Peace be with you,' said Jesus. Then He turned to Thomas and said, 'Put your finger in the wounds in my hands, and your hand in my side. Stop doubting, Thomas, and *believe!*'

Thomas answered, 'My Lord and my God!'

'You *believe because* you have seen me,' said Jesus. 'How happy will people *be* when they *believe* without *seeing* Me themselves.'

PICTURE PUZZLE

Only one of the five men on the right is a true match for the man in the box. Which one?
Put a circle round the right letter.

COUNT THE NAILS

Thomas didn't believe Jesus was alive until he felt the holes where the nails went in. Hidden in the picture are lots of nails. Can you find out how many there are?

Answer ______________

WORD PUZZLE

Fit the following words into the grid.

3	was	see	his	
4	died	down	feet	
5	Jesus	hands	nails	knelt
	touch	alive	peace	
6	people			
8	believed			
9	disciples			

BREAKFAST ON THE BEACH

Jesus appeared to His disciples early one morning. This is what happened:

Simon Peter wanted to go out fishing.

'I'm setting off now,' He told His friends. 'Does anyone want to come fishing with me?'

Six other disciples joined Him and they pushed the boat out on to the lake. It was still early in the morning. They put down their nets into the water and waited for the fish to come. But nothing happened. They did not catch a single fish.

Simon Peter looked up and saw a figure on the beach. They couldn't see who it was. The man called to Simon Peter.

'Throw your net on the other side of the boat and you will catch plenty of fish,' said the man.

So they threw their nets on the other side. At once the net became so full of fish that the fishermen could not pull it into the boat!

Suddenly one of the disciples knew who the man on the shore must be. It had to be Jesus!

They went to the shore and saw a charcoal fire there with some fish and some bread.

Jesus told them to bring some of the fresh fish to cook. 'Come and eat!' He said.

WORD PUZZLE

Choosing the correct words from below, rewrite the passage so that it makes sense.

right	**home**	**waited**	**disciples**	**Sea**	**catch**
fish	**shouted**	**tired**	**beach**	**caught**	**six**

One evening Peter and ______ of Jesus' other __________ went out on the ____ of Galilee to ______. They threw out their nets and ________. All night they waited, but they did not ______ a single fish. The fishermen were ______ and disappointed. As they turned to go ______ they saw a man on the ______.

'Have you ________ anything?' He ________.

'No,' they said.

'Throw your net on the ________ side of the boat,' said the man. 'Then you will catch some fish.'

SPOT THE STARFISH

How many starfish can you see hiding in the picture?

Answer ________

WORD QUIZ

The answers to these questions can be found hidden in the grid. But they don't always follow a straight line – the answers to questions 2 and 8 turn corners!

1) Apart from Peter, how many disciples went out to fish? ________
2) What was the sea called? ________
3) What did they throw out to sea? ________
4) How long did they wait to catch fish? ________
5) How many fish did the fishermen catch? ________
6) They were disappointed. How else did the fishermen feel? ________
7) Which side of the boat was the net thrown? ________
8) Where did Peter look to when he saw a man? ________
9) Who was the man Peter saw? ________
10 What was Jesus cooking over a fire? ________
11) What else did Jesus have to eat? ________
12) What was the meal Jesus ate with Peter? ________

S	E	A	O	F	X	S	J	B
L	I	L	A	G	I	T	R	A
E	E	H	J	D	S	E	I	L
S	B	K	A	N	A	N	G	L
O	U	E	P	K	O	F	H	N
M	R	S	F	N	I	K	T	I
B	V	A	E	S	B	E	A	G
C	S	X	H	J	Z	H	C	H
T	I	R	E	D	Y	T	R	T

JESUS GOES TO HEAVEN

After Jesus was resurrected from the dead, He stayed with His disciples for forty days.

Jesus ate and drank with His friends on many different occasions during this time and talked with them about God's kingdom.

When they met together, Jesus told them something very important that they must do.

'Don't leave Jerusalem,' He said, 'but wait for the special gift that I will leave you. You must wait for God's Holy Spirit to come. Then you will be filled with power and will be able to tell everyone about Me. You will want to make sure everyone knows about the things I have taught you, and about my death and resurrection, wherever they live in the world.'

Jesus' disciples asked Him many questions. They wanted to know if God's Kingdom was coming soon.

'Don't worry about these things,' said Jesus. 'You don't need to know the times or places for them.'

Then Jesus was taken up to heaven. A cloud hid Him from their sight as they watched.

Jesus' friends were still watching the sky when two men appeared next to them. They were dressed all in white.

'Why are you standing here looking up

at the sky?' they asked. 'Jesus will come back again in the same way as you saw Him go,' they promised.

Jesus' friends believed all that Jesus had told them. They waited in Jerusalem for the Holy Spirit, praying together.

They knew each other well. There was Peter, John, James and Andrew, Philip and Thomas, Bartholomew and Matthew, James, Simon and Judas. They chose another disciple, called Matthias, to be in their group.

Mary, Jesus' mother, and other women who loved Jesus, joined them to pray to God. About 120 people believed in Jesus at that time.

CAN YOU REMEMBER?

There are twelve things added to the larger picture, each taken from the stories about Jesus.
Can you find them all?
The smaller picture is there to help you.

WHICH STORY?

How much can you remember about the stories from the life of Jesus? The answers to these questions are all in the New Testament section of this book.

1 Name the town where Jesus was born. ______

2 What gifts did the wise men bring to Jesus? ______

3 How many disciples did Jesus have? ______

4 Name the lake where Jesus calmed a storm. ______

5 Who asked Jesus to heal his daughter? ______

6 What did Jesus use to feed more than 5000 people? ______

7 Who helped the wounded man on the road to Jericho? ______

8 Why did Bartimaeus want Jesus to help him? ______

9 What job did Zacchaeus do? ______

10 What happened three days after Jesus was crucified? ______

THE GOOD NEWS OF JESUS

On the day of Pentecost, Jesus' disciples and all the other believers were meeting together in a room.

Suddenly there was a noise like a strong wind blowing. The noise filled the whole house. Tongues of fire touched everyone in the room and every one was filled with the Holy Spirit.

It was just as Jesus had promised.

The believers found they could suddenly speak in all kinds of languages! Many people in Jerusalem from other countries could understand what they were saying.

Peter told the crowds all about Jesus. He told them about how Jesus had done amazing things, healed people and shown God's power. He had been put to death on a cross but he had come alive again!

'Turn away from doing wrong,' said Peter. 'Believe in Jesus and be baptised. You will be forgiven and you will receive God's gift of the Holy Spirit!'

About three thousand people believed and were baptised that same day and joined the disciples.

Jesus' friends and the new believers wanted to tell more people the good news.

Some believers travelled to other countries, many faced great danger, and some never came home again. But they were all filled with God's love for the people they met.

They wanted to share the good news of Jesus and tell everyone about God's wonderful Kingdom.

What's Not Right?

There are twelve things wrong with the picture below. Can you spot the mistakes?

Definitions

Can you match up seven of the following words with their definitions opposite?

SILLY BAPTISM SHARE AMAZED FEAST PENTECOST DISCIPLE SUPPER SINNING CONFESS

1) Admit to having done something wrong

2) When the descent of the Holy Spirit came upon the believers

3) Someone who follows and learns

4) A sign that a person has been forgiven their sins

5) To be filled with astonishment

6) Breaking God's laws

7) A grand meal for many people to celebrate an occasion

LANGUAGES

Can you understand what the crowd is saying. And what three languages are they speaking?

Mary's Baby Pages 102-103

• The passage should read:

Mary lived in the little **town** of **Nazareth**. She was **planning** to marry a **carpenter** named **Joseph**. One day the **Angel Gabriel** came to **Mary**. '**God** is pleased with you,' said Gabriel. 'You are going to have a **baby**. He will be called the **son** of God. He will be a great King like **David**.'

• The answers are shown in the grid.

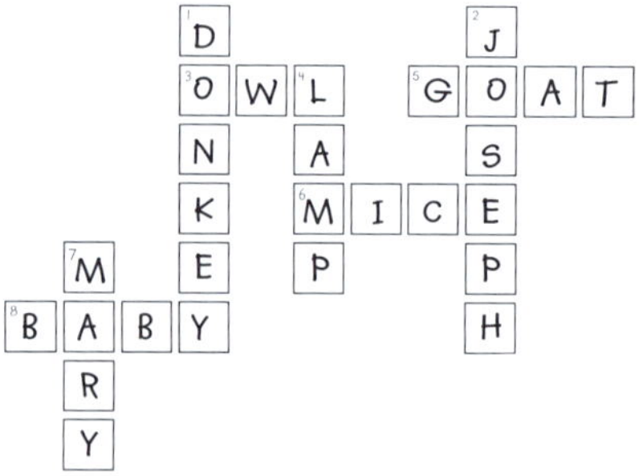

The Angel and the Shepherds Pages 106-107

• The answers are circled on the picture.

• The answers are shown in the grid.

W	A	S					
A	C	H	E				
A	N	G	E	L			
P	E	A	C	E	F	U	L
W	H	A	T				
M	A	N	G	E	R		
F	I	R	E				
T	I	R	E	D			
S	A	I	D				

• The shaded squares spell:
SHEPHERDS

The Journey of the Wise Men Page 110-111

• The answers are circled on the grid.

• The answers are shown in bold type

PRHU**BETHLEHEM**VXB**BOY**AOAJHUIFK**HEROD**LOPNBHF**JESUS**
BVYTUEKS**JERUSALEM**BVHFYITASL**MYRRH**OPLFD**WISEMEN**
STARLODJF**GOLD**KORF**MARY**ICKPKENSE**PALACE**XME**KING**W

• The unused letters spell:
THE JOURNEY OF THE WISE MEN

The Four Fishermen Pages 114-115

• The letters spell: DISCIPLES

• The matching pieces are: 1, 3, 6, 7 and 9.

Jesus meets Matthew Pages 118-119

• The decoded questions are:

What was Matthew? A tax collector.
Where did Jesus eat? Matthew's house.
Who grumbled? The teachers of the law.
What did Matthew become? A disciple.

• The answers are circled on the picture.

The Four Kind Friends Page 122-123

• The answers are: A **False**, B **False**, C **True**, D **False**, E **False**, F **True**, G **False**, H **True**.

The Story of the Two Houses Pages 126-127

• The missing words are:

Once Jesus told a **story** about a **wise** man who wanted to **build** a **house**.

'Where shall I build it?' the **man** wondered. 'Shall I build it near the **sea**? Shall I build it near the **river**? Shall I build it in a **field**? No! I will build it on solid **rock**.'

The wise man began to build. He worked **hard**. He worked for a **long** time. When his house was **finished** he was **pleased**.

• The missing vowels are:

'If **you** listen **to** my words **and** **obey** them, **you** will **be** **like** **a** wise man who **built** his **house** **upon** **a** rock.'

• You should live in the house of the **hard working** man.

The Big Storm Pages 130-131

• The completed words are:

DISCIPLES, HIGHER, LOWER, JESUS, SEA, LAKE, ROCKED, PILLOW, WENT, SHOOK, AWAKE, DROWN, WAVES, STORM, WIND, CALM, EXCITED, FAST, REST, BOAT, HELP, CROSS, HOWLING, SINK, STOOD, AFRAID, IMPORTANT

H	L	S	E	L	P	I	C	S	I	D	B
K	O	R	Y	X	R	E	H	G	I	H	O
S	W	W	E	Y	C	D	I	A	R	F	A
E	E	R	L	S	P	I	L	L	O	W	T
V	R	A	O	I	T	S	T	Z	O	W	N
A	P	W	K	C	N	J	S	E	E	I	A
W	F	A	W	O	K	G	E	O	D	N	T
L	A	K	E	S	P	E	M	S	R	D	R
A	S	E	N	H	J	H	D	L	U	C	O
E	T	S	T	O	O	D	S	W	A	S	P
S	I	N	K	O	N	W	O	R	D	C	M
P	L	E	H	K	S	T	O	R	M	M	I

• The answers are circled in the grid.

• **13** people are in the boat.

You can see **1** oar.

2 people are wearing stripes.

5 have their heads covered.

2 are pulling on the oar.

The total is **23**.

• A, D and E sailed in the boat

The Girl Who Came Back to Life Pages 134-135

• The correct spellings are:

Jairus, Doctors, Please, Daughter, Believe, Messenger, Could, Room, Miracle and **Twelve**

• The decoded questions are:

Who was dying? Jairus' daughter.

Who did Jesus heal? A woman.

Who went with Jesus? Peter, John and James.

How old was the girl? Twelve.

The Living Bread Pages 138-139

• The answers are circled on the picture on the right.

• The answers are circled and numbered on the picture below.

The Good Neighbour Pages 142-143

• The answers are circled on the picture.

• The text should read:

'Just then a **third** man, a **Samaritan**, came down the **road**. As soon as he saw the wounded man, he rushed up to him. "What happened to you?" he asked. "Let me **help you**."

'The **Samaritan** gave him something to **drink**, bandaged his **wounds**, and lifted him **on to his own donkey**. He took the man to **an inn** where the **Samaritan** paid the **innkeeper** two **silver coins** to look after him.

The Story of the Lost Sheep Pages 146-147

- 3 + 2 x 4 + 2 = 22.
2 x 6 + 2 x 3 = 42.
6 + 6 x 3 = 36.
- The shepherd had **100** sheep.
100 - 1 = **99**
100 x 1/2 = **50**
100 - 10 + 5 = **95**
100 - 20 + 15 = **95**
100 - 70 - 5 = **25**
100 - 40 - 5 = **55**
- The correct path the shepherd takes is shown in the maze.

The Man Who Could Not See Pages 150-151

- Bartimaeus could see figures **A, C, D, E, G,** and **I.**
- The secret message should read:

When I need help, Lord Jesus, remind me to ask you.

- Bartimaeus asked Jesus: **'I want to see!'**

The Little Tax Collector Pages 154-155

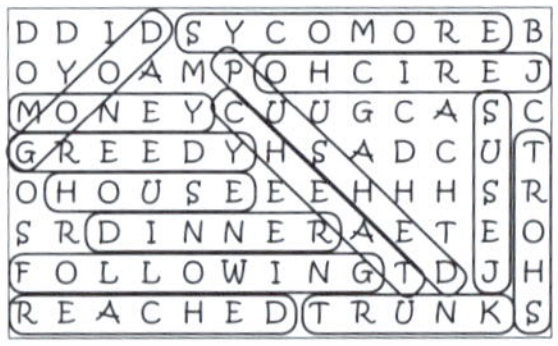

The words read: Short, Reached, Following, House, Sycomore, Money, Jesus, Dinner, Good, Trunk, Pushed, Greedy, Jericho, Cheat. And are ringed in the grid.

The King on a Donkey Pages 158-159

- The decoded message should read:

This is my body which I will give up for you. This is my blood which I will shed for you.

- The differences are circled.

The correct path is shown.

Jesus is Crucified Page 162-163

- The small wooden crosses are circled on the picture.
- The answers to the Word Puzzle are:

1) Arrested	5) Paid	9) Entrance
2) Wrong	6) Stumbled	10) Hit
3) Angry	7) Heavy	11) Thought
3) Wished	8) Near	12) Nailed

Jesus is Alive Pages 166-167

- The differences are circled on the picture.

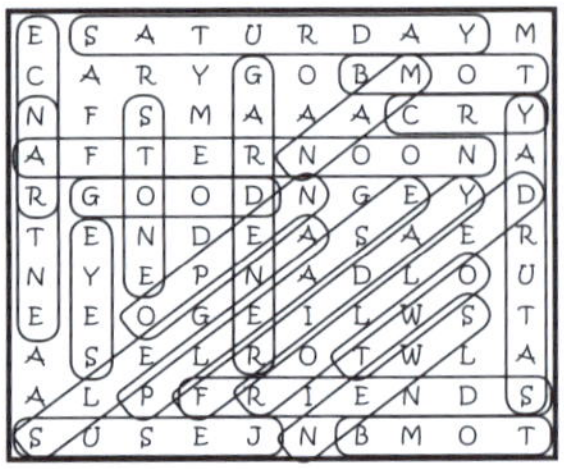

- The words are circled in the grid
- The important person is **Mary of Magdala**
- The two repeated words are **Saturday** and **Tomb.**
- The pairs of words are:
back - front, happy - sad, alive - dead, enemies - friends, outside - inside, wasn't - was, entrance - exit, full - empty, standing - sitting, something - nothing, cried - laughed, light - dark.
- The words that shouldn't be there are: **side, bad, clean, down**

Thomas Believes Pages 170-171

• Figure D is the correct match for the man in the box.

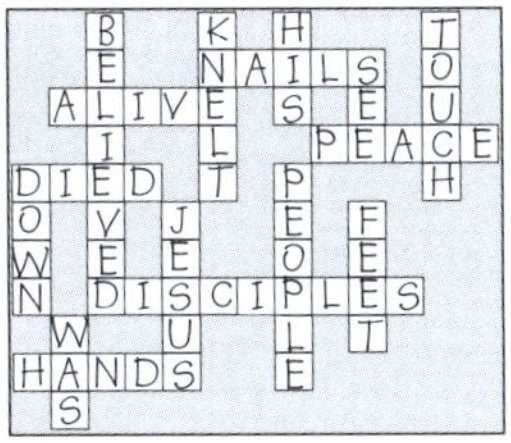

• There are **ten** nails all circled on the picture.

• The completed grid is shown at the right.

Breakfast on the Beach Pages 174-175

• The passage should read: One evening Peter and **six** of Jesus' other **disciples** went out on the **Sea** of Galilee to **fish**. They threw out their nets and **waited**. All night they waited, but they did not **catch** a single fish. The fishermen were **tired** and disappointed. As they turned to go **home** they saw a man on the **beach**.
'Have you **cought** anything,' he **shouted**.
'No,' they said.
'Throw your net on the **right** side of the boat,' said the man. 'Then you will catch some fish.'

• There are **twelve** starfish circled in the picture.

• 1) **Six**
2) **Sea of Galilee**
3) **Nets**
4) **All night**
5) **None**
6) **Tired**
7) **Right**
8) **Beach**
9) **Jesus**
10) **Fish**
11) **Bread**
12) **Breakfast**

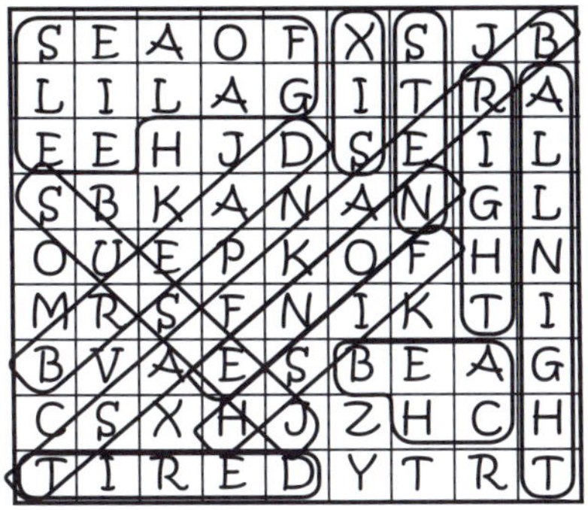

Jesus goes to Heaven Pages 178-179

• The twelve things are circled on the picture.

• 1) Bethlehem
2) Gold, Frankincense and Myrrh
3) Twelve
4) Sea of Galilee.
5) Jairus
6) 5 loaves and 2 fish.
7) The good Samaritan.
8) He asked Jesus to cure his blindness and help him to see.
9) A tax collector.
10) He rose from the dead.

The Good News of Jesus Pages 182-183

• 1) Confess, 2) Pentecost, 3) Disciple, 4) Baptism, 5) Amazed, 6) Sinning, 7) Feast

• They are all saying Hello
Guten Tag is **German,** Hola is **Spanish,** Bonjour is **French**

• The twelve wrong things are circled on the picture.

BIBLE STORIES CAN BE FOUND AS FOLLOWS:

OLD TESTAMENT

The Beautiful Garden Genesis 1:1-31

The Enemy in the Garden Genesis 2:8 – 3:24

The Triple-Decker Boat Genesis 6:9 – 7:24

Rain, Rain, and More Rain Genesis 8:1 – 9:17

Abram's Journey Genesis 12:1-8

A Gift from God Genesis 15:4-5; 17:4-16: 18:1-15; 21:1-3

Jacob Plays a Trick Genesis 25:21-34; 27:1-45

Joseph's Jealous Brothers Genesis 37:1-11

A Slave in Egypt Genesis 37:12-36; 39:1 – 46:30

The Baby in the Basket Exodus 2:1-10

Let My People Go Exodus 3:1 – 12:51

The Great Escape Exodus 13:17 – 15:21

Joshua and the Battle of Jericho Joshua 1:1-6; 5:13 – 6:20

Samuel's Sleepless Night 1 Samuel 3:1-21

The Shepherd Boy 1 Samuel 16:1-23

David and the Giant 1 Samuel 17:1-50

God Takes Care of Elijah 1 Kings 17:1-16

Fire from Heaven 1 Kings 18:16-45

Naaman and the Little Servant Girl 2 Kings 5:1-15

Daniel in the Lions' Den Daniel 6:1-24

Jonah Runs Away Jonah 1:1 – 3:10

NEW TESTAMENT

Bible Quiz

Now that you have read all the stories and completed all the puzzles, see if you can answer the following quiz questions.

There is one question for every story in the book. Look back at the stories if you need help.

1 What was the name of the garden God made?

____

2 How did Adam and Eve feel when they had eaten the fruit? ______________________________

3 What did God send to wash the earth clean?

____

4 Which bird brought back an olive branch?

____

5 Name the land that God gave to Abram.

____

6 Name the twin boys born to Isaac and Rebecca.

____

7 Which son did Isaac bless before he died?

____

8 How many children did Jacob have? ______________

9 Where was Joseph taken to be a slave?

____

10 Which river were Israelite babies thrown into?

____

11 What message did God give to Moses for the king of Egypt? ______________________________

12 Who appeared as a pillar of fire by night to lead the Israelites? ______________________________

13 Who led the Israelites when Moses died?

____

14 Who was Samuel's mother? ______________

15 Which king did David play his harp for? __________

____

16 What did David use to kill the giant? __________

____

17 Which king was angry with Elijah? __________

____

18 Where did Elijah hold a contest? __________

____

19 Who told Naaman to wash seven times in the River Jordan? ______________________________

20 How did Daniel break the king's rule? __________

____

21 What did God do when the people of Nineveh said sorry? ______________________________

22 Name the angel who brought a message to Mary.

____

23 Who came to visit the baby Jesus on the night He was born? ____________________

24 What gifts did the wise men bring? ____________________

____

25 Name the first four disciples. ____________________

____

26 What was Matthew doing when Jesus called him?

____

27 What did the four men do so Jesus would heal their friend. ____________________

____

28 On what did the wise man build his house in Jesus' story? ____________________

29 What happened when Jesus spoke to the wind and waves? ____________________

30 Why did Jairus need Jesus' help? ____________________

____

31 Who told Jesus about the boy with five loaves and two fish? ____________________

32 In Jesus' story of the good Samaritan, which road was the man travelling? ____________________

____

33 What did the shepherd do when he found that one of his sheep was lost? ____________________

____

34 Why could Bartimaeus not see Jesus? ____________________

____

35 What did Zacchaeus do after Jesus had come to his house? ____________________

____

____

36 What did the people wave when Jesus entered Jerusalem? ____________________

37 What did the cruel soldiers put on Jesus' head?

____

38 Why was Jesus not in the tomb where He was buried? ____________________

____

39 Which disciple could not believe Jesus had risen from the dead? ____________________

40 How many disciples were in the boat when Jesus called to them after His resurrection? ____________________

41 Where did Jesus go forty days after His resurrection? ____________________

42 What happened on the Day of Pentecost?

____

The answers are on page 192.

Bible Quiz Answers

1 The Garden of Eden.
2 Guilty.
3 Flood.
4 A dove.
5 Canaan.
6 Esau and Jacob.
7 Jacob.
8 Thirteen.
9 Egypt.
10 The River Nile.
11 'Let My people go!'
12 God.
13 Joshua.
14 Hannah.
15 King Saul.
16 A stone and a sling.
17 King Ahab.
18 Mount Carmel.
19 Elisha.
20 He worshipped God.
21 God forgave them.
22 The angel Gabriel.
23 Some shepherds.
24 Gold, frankincense and myrrh.
25 Peter, Andrew, James and John.
26 Collecting taxes.
27 They made a hole in the roof.
28 On a rock.
29 They were still and calm.
30 His daughter was dying.
31 Andrew.
32 The road from Jerusalem to Jericho.
33 He left the other sheep to look for it.
34 He was blind.
35 He gave half his money to the poor and gave back four times the money he had stolen by cheating people.
36 Palm branches.
37 A crown of thorns.
38 God had raised Jesus from the dead.
39 Thomas.
40 Seven.
41 To His Father in heaven.
42 The Holy Spirit came.